Grandfather's Microscope

Grandfather's Microscope

H. Mei Liu

Copyright © 2002 by H. Mei Liu.

Library of Congress Number: 2002095093
ISBN: Hardcover   1-4010-7830-3
                 Softcover   1-4010-7829-X

All rights reserved. No part of this book may be reproduced or transmitted in any form or by any means, electronic or mechanical, including photocopying, recording, or by any information storage and retrieval system, without permission in writing from the copyright owner.

This book was printed in the United States of America.

To order additional copies of this book, contact:
Xlibris Corporation
1-888-795-4274
www.Xlibris.com
Orders@Xlibris.com

Contents

Prologue
Deborah Wang (2nd daughter) 11

Chapter 1
Dragon Boat Ghost 19

Chapter 2
Three-inch Golden Lily 31

Chapter 3
Golden Rice Bowl 42

Chapter 4
Hunan, my ancestral home 58

Chapter 5
Song Girl's Ignorance 66

Chapter 6
The Struggle 87

Chapter 7
Under the Peach Blossoms 104

Chapter 8
Exodus 113

Chapter 9
My ABC Daughter 130

Chapter 10
Becoming a neuropathologist 142

Chapter 11
Kung Fu, Grasshopper and Ramon y Cajal 151

Chapter 12
Feng Shui 162

Chapter 13
The Yale Dream 175

Chapter 14
The East Wind 189

Chapter 15
The Women Warriors 202

Chapter 16
The Martyr 215

Chapter 17
Yuan, the spiritual link 234

Chapter 18
The Soul Bridge 240

DEDICATION

*Dedicated to the memory of
my grandfather and his dreams*

Acknowledgments

I would like to thank my two daughters, Pamela Wang Anderson and Deborah Wang Ferguson for their help in writing this book. This is truly a family project. I have finally fulfilled a promise I made to them long ago when they were children that one day they would get the chance to know their mother and their roots.

My daughters not only encouraged me to write my memoir, but they each contributed an insightful chapter. In addition, Deborah edited the text, and Pamela helped me design the book cover, retouched the photographs and set up a website.

I am indebted to my sister Lan for always being my inspiration. Her article "Grandfather's Yale Dream" set an example for me to follow. Thanks to her daughter Tong who helped me with pinyin spelling, information about family members, and helpful suggestions about artwork. Thanks also to my cousins in the Xie family, Xiaowen, Zhongwen and Yulan who have contributed valuable information about the life of their parents, my Thin Aunt and her husband.

Thanks to Virgie Stenson, Leslie Beauchamp Wang and Phyllis Charles for their editorial help. To Virgie especially, I owe many thanks for her genuine friendship and invaluable advice.

I want to thank the University of Hawaii for allowing me

to audit their writing courses, and Professor Philip Daimon for getting me started on autobiographical writing.

Finally, I want to thank Professor Wang Yanzhi of Hunan Medical College for composing the poem and writing the scroll of calligraphy which appears on the book cover. For interested readers, here is the translation:

> Although you have traveled ten thousand li
> A thread of love binds you to your ancestral home
> The place where Dongting Lake meets River Li
> Is where the talent of Hunan calls home
> Don't say this talent has gone away
> Praise echoes around the world for Mei

Prologue

DEBORAH WANG (2ND DAUGHTER)

In May of 1990, while I was a correspondent in National Public Radio's Hong Kong Bureau, I received a phone call from my editors in Washington asking me to do a story about a French ship that had just arrived in Taiwan.

A group of expatriate Chinese dissidents and their French patrons had boarded an old cargo ship and set sail towards China. They intended to anchor at some nearby port and broadcast pro-democracy propaganda to the mainland. It was a foolish idea, really, since no country had given them any indication that their pirate radio ship would be welcome in its ports. But they set off anyway, hoping to persuade Taiwan, China's archrival, to agree to their presence. The ship was called "Deese dé la Démocratie" and boasted on its bow a replica of the statue "Goddess of Democracy," the symbol of the ill-fated student movement in Tiananmen Square.

When I arrived at bustling Chiang Kai-shek International Airport in Taipei, I was met by my mother Mei Liu. It had been months since I had seen her last. I was struck this time by how much she had aged. She had been one of those timeless people, always looked decades younger than she really was. She would joke about being perpetually twenty-nine and yet there always seemed some truth to the boast (she allowed the twenty-nine to slip a decade or so in her later years). Although she seldom played sports as an adult, she constantly recalled the athletic achievements of her youth, and made a point to keep reasonably fit and strong to the fingertips. But now the veneer of youth had begun to fade, and my mother was looking her age, which shouldn't have been much of a surprise. After all she was sixty years old. Time had finally begun to catch up with her.

Then again, perhaps it was a matter of context. I had always been used to seeing my mother in her beautiful Victorian house in a leafy part of Providence, Rhode Island, lording over her gourmet kitchen, battling the weeds in her garden, curling up on her couch with her three cats, all of whom she claimed to despise and yet who managed to share her home for over a decade. But now that life was over. She had traded it for a tiny apartment in an anonymous concrete block in polluted Taipei. Whereas she was once master of her domain, she was now an old lady living alone in a foreign land, entirely out of her element. Yet my mother had taken that on at an age when most people are happily settling into the easy, carefree years of their retirement. Why she had chosen to do this, she was never able to give a very convincing explanation. All we knew was one day she just woke up, quit her teaching job at Brown University, put her house on the market, threw away her antique furniture and most of the collective memorabilia of our lives, disposed of her by now elderly cats, and bought a one way ticket to a place none of us had ever been.

Her sudden decision to up and take off was greeted within the family by a generalized feeling of horror.

"How is she going to live, all by herself on the other side of the world?" asked my brother, Peter, a geophysicist, and one of those careful people who balances his checkbook after every check he writes. My sister, Doctor Pam, was more to the point. "I think she's losing her marbles," she said. She envisioned Mom becoming a bag lady, dragging around her Samsonite suitcases and begging for small change on the streets of Taipei.

I was the only one who even vaguely sympathized with her. I had once had the same urges, at the age of 19, when I was a junior in college. I had taken off in the same direction, ending up on the other side of the bamboo curtain. For me, it was a journey motivated entirely by the need for self-discovery, to find out in some metaphysical way who I was. For a year, I lived and breathed China, learned the language, wandered the countryside, trying to uncover my roots. I wrote endless, tortured letters to my family but never once called home.

My Mom was not given that luxury. When she was young, she had been preoccupied by a host of much more pressing issues. Who had time for self-discovery? She was trying to survive! The way I figured it, Mom was living a kind of delayed adolescence. She was embarking on a rite of passage that is every red-blooded American teenager's right. Good for her, I thought. A little self-reflection never hurt anybody.

Later, when I landed the job with National Public Radio and was dispatched to nearby Hong Kong, Pam sighed with relief. "Good, now you can keep an eye on her!" she declared. So Mom was on her voyage of self-discovery, and I was her chaperone.

When I told Mom that I would have to travel north to see the ship anchored in Keelung Harbor, her face lit up. She asked if she could tag along, and I said sure. Throughout the hour-long taxi ride, my normally taciturn mother kept peppering the driver with questions. She wanted to know if he remembered a certain former mayor of Keelung surnamed Xie.

"Oh sure," said the driver. "He was the best mayor this city ever had."

"Is he still alive by chance?" she asked. There was a hint of hope in her voice.

"No, he died a long time ago, must be fifteen or twenty years now. See over there?" The driver pointed to a small hill to the south. "The mayor was buried up there so he could look over the city forever."

My mother peered out towards the hillside, straining to see, and then let out a sigh. I asked her why she was so interested in this man.

"The mayor saved my life forty years ago," she replied.

I was under deadline and preoccupied with my story, so somehow I let this moment of confession slip by. Mom grew silent as I scribbled in my notebook. We reached the port and the hulking red bow of the ship loomed before us. I boarded the ship across a narrow gangway to cover a news conference by the ship's crew, while my Mom disappeared among the crowds at the dock. At some point someone took photographs of us standing by the ship, the only tangible memory I have of that day.

The report I filed was not a big news item, and I soon put it out of my mind. It wasn't until years later that I began to understand the impact the visit to Keelung Harbor had on my mother. The sight of that rusty ship going nowhere had unlocked in her some deeply suppressed memories. My strong, quiet, tough-minded mother, always a problem solver, who never looked back, embarked on a voyage of self-discovery that would consume much of her later life. Little by little, she began to unravel the threads of her past.

The tales she tells are by turns amusing and painful. All point to a life of extraordinary determination and complexity. In telling them, she feels she has brought some order and closure to her life. And she has illuminated for her children a history that we hardly imagined existed.

Mei Liu

When I was eighteen years old, a college student in China, my fate was laid out before me by a stranger.

GRANDFATHER'S MICROSCOPE

One Sunday, a long lost friend of my father's came to our house to borrow money for his sick wife who needed medical attention. This friend was a poet, a calligrapher and a philosopher of sorts, but had never held a regular job. Without hesitation, my father lent his friend the year-end bonus he had just received from his company. It was money badly needed by his own ten children. As far as I know, the loan was never paid back. In gratitude, the friend offered to tell my fortune, along with my sister Lan's. We were the two oldest children, and the repository of our parents' grandest dreams.

The fortuneteller was sitting on the rattan sofa between my parents. Lan and I were sitting by the table. The man was middle-aged, delicately built and looked scholarly in his Mandarin gown and gold-rimmed spectacles. He took a long time to examine our eight letters: the hour, date, month and year of our births. He started by saying that my parents would be able to share the *fu*, good fortune, which Lan and I had in our fate. Everyone in the room sighed with relief. Then the fortuneteller looked more closely at my eight letters. His face changed, something in my fate alarmed him.

"She will have an unusual life, see here?" The man pointed to something he had written on the paper. "Her life will be full of toil and unrest. She will have ups and downs, every twenty years a cycle."

The room was silent. Everyone was waiting.

"Ay-yah! When she is twenty years old, her fate will be like a lonely raft adrift in the rapids with danger at every turn," the fortuneteller continued. My father was frowning, my mother looked puzzled. I felt seasick already. That's only two years into the future!

After a long pause while I held my breath, the man said: "And then—when she is forty years old, there will be a second disaster." I was secretly relieved that I didn't have to die at the age of twenty. "She will come to face her evil star and a domestic calamity."

I looked at my parents. This time, it was my mother's turn to frown; she seemed to have perceived the nature of the calamity. The fortuneteller continued: "When she reaches sixty, she will have the biggest change . . . . fast wind and big waves . . . ."

He hesitated as though he was withholding some important information. My parents did not encourage him to continue. Although the man had used the word change and not danger or disaster, I had a premonition that the "big change" signified a final act, the end of my life. But I did not let it worry me, that would be a long, long way into the future.

It was not until I was in my fifties when the fortuneteller's predictions came back to haunt me. I began to hear the clock ticking and feel the approach of my impending mortality. I was also struggling with a growing feeling of rootlessness, of "not belonging."

I suppose age brings its own compulsions. Those locked-away memories began to resurface, almost on their own. I realized that my own past was a remarkable adventure set against a peculiar family background during the most turbulent years in Chinese history. Many of the threads that I thought were broken continued to exist and to exert their influence. I felt the need to connect them, to make some sense of how I have become who I am, and to understand the cycle of dreams, and broken promises, that seem to recur in my life.

So much became clear during the visit to Keelung harbor on that fine day in May of 1990. As I watched my daughter, dressed in T-shirt and blue jeans, going up the gangway of the Goddess of Democracy, my heart swelled with pride.

Lucky girl! I could not help thinking, and lucky mother!

A soft mist rolled in front of me and blurred my vision. Through the mist I saw a young woman walking down the gangway. She was wearing a royal blue Mandarin gown and carrying all her worldly possessions stuffed into a small suitcase. The girl looked remarkably like my daughter, but far from being the confident young professional, this girl was in a daze, full of fear and confusion. She had left behind family, friends, everything she knew, to sneak aboard a ship bound for Taiwan....

A loud horn blast from a ship jarred me out of my reverie. I realized with a start I was seeing the ghost of my past which lived undimmed in my memory. The voyage seemed so remote, yet so recent. Here, right here on this dock, was where I got off the boat that was carrying one of the last loads of refugees out of China. The time was May 1949.

It has been both painful and joyous to relive the past and to explore the vast unknown space within myself. Now I have come to realize that in one's sunset years, the past sometimes burns more brightly than the present. I feel obliged to write it down and leave it to my children and their children, the extraordinary events that have crowded into my life.

Mei at Keelung harbor, Taiwan, in front of the ship "Deesse dé la Démocratie." 1990. Photograph by Deborah.

Deborah at the Keelung pier, Taiwan,
interviewing people who have gathered to watch
the ship "Deesse dé la Démocratie." 1990.
Photograph by Mei.

* Note on spelling of Chinese names and places: I have adopted the universally used pinyin system except for the names that had already been well established :Yangtze River, Keelung harbor, Peking University, Peking opera, Sun Yat-sen, Chiang Kai-shek (Jiang Jieshi in pinyin), Chiang Ching-kuo, my first name Hsiang (Xiang in pinyin), my grandfather's name Hsia (Xia in pinyin), and Hsiang Ya medical school.

Chapter 1

DRAGON BOAT GHOST

It was October 10, 1953 when I first set foot on the land of my dreams. I had arrived in San Francisco after a nineteen-day transpacific voyage aboard the S.S. President Wilson, reeling from seasickness, and carrying a small suitcase that contained my newly acquired medical diploma and a large volume of Grey's Human Anatomy. It was like landing on Mars! I was lost amidst a sea of "foreign devils," all speaking a language that I didn't understand. I somehow managed to communicate to a kind-hearted gentleman, who directed me to the railway station where I boarded a train to Rochester, N.Y., my final destination. I was twenty-four years old, and about to embark on my medical career.

My new home, Rochester General Hospital, was like a wonderland to me. I was immediately in awe of the elegant old buildings, the crisp uniforms of the medical staff, the air of authority, knowledge, and promise that seemed to permeate the very walls of the old institution. Everything was new and exciting. I was desperate to learn everything I could, not just about medicine, but also about the language, the food, how Americans lived their lives, how they spent their time. I wanted so badly to fit in, to understand what was expected of me. To my surprise, I found that there were quite a few foreigners among the residents, from all over the world: England, Germany, Italy, the Netherlands, Turkey, Korea and China. It was like an international student assembly. I was relieved I was not the only one who was struggling to understand.

During the first few months, I could hardly communicate, despite the fact that I had studied English for many years in China. I had no difficulty understanding the medical dialogue. As a medical student in Taiwan, I studied English textbooks, and wrote medical histories and progress notes in English. My problem was with the everyday conversation, particularly the American slang. I would answer most questions with the phrase, "pardon me?" It was so embarrassing that I often would play deaf and dumb, or just smile and nod.

I had come to Rochester to take up a residency in pathology. I would learn to make diagnoses on tissues that the surgeons took out from live patients or from patients after death. At the time, there was a shortage of pathologists at US hospitals. Most people who choose to become doctors prefer to deal with living, breathing patients, rather than tissues and cadavers. And most consider laboratory work a lonely job. The pathologists are regarded as "doctors of death," not real doctors. As a result, positions in the pathology department were often taken up by foreigners, who were eager for any work. And since there was little or no contact with patients, it didn't matter how well you could speak English. It seemed the logical fit for me.

But it wasn't long before I began to question my choice of specialties.

My first assignment was to watch a senior resident performing an autopsy, the most routine of procedures for any pathologist.

When I entered the autopsy room, a naked corpse was laid out on the stainless steel table. Our senior resident, dressed in surgical attire, was ready to begin. My first impression of Paul was that he looked like Gary Cooper, one of the few Americans with whom I was familiar. But far from the tough Gary Copper image on the screen, Paul was laid back and sensitive. He had had two years of training in surgery, but he didn't like it. His personality was not suited for surgery, he said. When he did his 6-month pathology rotation (mandatory for all surgical residents), he decided to switch.

As a former surgeon, Paul was adept with a scalpel. First, he made a smooth, Y-shaped incision across the chest and down the center of the abdomen. I braced myself for blood to gush out of the wound. But most of the blood had already coagulated, and the incision remained clean. He then used a larger, blunt knife to separate the skin and muscle from the rib cage and the sternum. Then a bone cutter was used to crack the ribs on both sides, so he could lift off the sternum to expose the internal organs. Once he had opened up a large hole in front of the body, he began to eviscerate, according to what pathologists call the Virchow method, which means taking the organs out one by one. Nowadays, most pathologists use the Rochitansky method of taking the organs out en block.

First, he freed the intestines, by slicing the mesentery, the fatty connections to the back of the body cavity. Then he went for the heart. As he grasped the heart in his hand and sliced it open, I felt my heart squeezing tight in my chest. I knew the patient was dead and couldn't care less one way or another, but still it seemed to me like a terrible violation. Although I was forcing myself to concentrate on the work, the sight of the bloody organs, the unpleasant smell of flesh, blood and intestine, and the strong formalin fumes made me ill. I found myself holding my breath throughout the procedure, trying to control my nausea.

When the procedure was finished, I bolted out the door in search of air. At that moment, I wondered how I would ever be able to do this for a living.

And then there were those recurrent nightmares!

In my dreams, I would be standing over a body, ready to begin work, and just as I was plunging the knife into the chest or holding the heart in my hands, the corpse would spring upright! I would be paralyzed with terror, unable to decide whether to drop the knife and run or knock the corpse out cold. Then I would wake with my heart pounding and covered in sweat.

I blamed my nightmares on old Charlie, the morgue attendant.

Charlie was Irish, an old bachelor, about sixty. He was short, slightly built and always dressed in the same wrinkled white shirt and navy-blue cotton pants. He would show up at work with red-rimmed blurry eyes, reeling across the floor.

"Morning Charlie, how are you today?" I would ask him.

"Oh-h-h, not so good, Doc, my stomach is bothering me," he would say, burping and grunting.

"Go see a doctor!" I told him.

I was genuinely concerned about his health. Where I came from, such symptoms were usually caused by ulcer or cancer of the stomach. In China, malnutrition was the problem, not alcoholism. In fact I had never seen a drunkard before.

I felt sorry for the old man, who was poor and sick all the time. Charlie was friendly towards me, but I felt uneasy when his lingering hands patted me on the back. He would lean so close I could smell the staleness of his breath. I was trying to adapt to a new culture in a country where public hugging and kissing were commonplace. These were codes of conduct of which I was utterly unfamiliar. I dismissed Charlie as a typical friendly American until the day I caught him in a strange act.

I was working by the table, which had been cleaned after an earlier autopsy. I took out a Mason jar and spread its contents, tissue slices hardened in formalin, on a cork board. Using a scalpel, I trimmed the tissues into neat, thin squares and fitted them into cassettes to be processed overnight in an automatic machine, the Technicon. The following morning, the tissues would be made into paraffin blocks, thinly sliced, stained with dye and made ready for microscopic examination.

While bending over the table, I was vaguely aware of Charlie puttering around me. He was sharpening knives on a whetstone and wiping the table with a sponge. When my work was done, I turned around to place the jar back on the shelf behind me. That's when I saw Charlie's face pressed against the floor.

I was dressed in a two-piece white uniform. The top had a wrap-around high collar with buttons down the left side, and the skirt was of medium length and width. As I bent over the autopsy table, the starched skirt stuck out in the back like a hoop. I was aware of a scrapping noise behind me and thought Charlie was mopping the floor. As it turned out, he was on all fours with his face turned to peek up my skirt.

I was dumbfounded!

Charlie quickly scampered to his feet and slunk away.

Mei at work as a second-year resident in Pathology at Rochester General Hospital, Rochester, N.Y. 1955.

The incident was so embarrassing to me that I could not bring myself to tell anyone about it. I was afraid that, with my clumsy English, I might say the wrong words and make a fool of myself. From that day on, I kept an iron face and a safe distance from Charlie. When I was on night call and the hospital operator notified me of an impending autopsy, I would tell her not to bother notifying the morgue attendant, I would do it alone.

As a former tomboy and athlete, I was in much better shape than Charlie and could easily have defended myself. But I didn't want to be put on the spot. I always had a healthy respect for my own temperament and knew what I was capable of doing when my survival instinct was put to the test. I had no desire to see my name in the next day's paper, with the headline: "Murder In The Morgue."

The morgue was the loneliest place in the hospital. It was located at the far end of the basement, past the maintenance and engineering departments, the furnace room, the electricity, plumbing, laundry, autoclave, and supply rooms. At night, the brightly-lit corridors were totally deserted and eerily quiet, the only noise was the hissing steam in the overhead pipes.

And yet here I was, a young woman just off the boat, learning to make a life for myself in this strange subterranean world. As I walked the basement corridors, I could sense the danger lurking behind the morgue door: an amorphous dark cavern brewing with ancient terrors, recent dangers and nameless fears. But still I had to force myself to enter that room, lock the door behind me, and turn to face the naked corpse on the table.

Why had I allowed myself to get into a situation like this? As a child, I had suffered from a morbid fear of ghosts! Ever since a ghost nearly snatched my mother away, my fear of the other world had become so severe that my maternal grandmother, Nai Nai, had to tie a ghost-repelling coin around my neck. How I wished I had Nai Nai's magic coin on me when I was alone with a corpse in the morgue at night!

I did learn, in a manner I could not explain, to curb my fears and concentrate on the tasks at hand. For me, when I put on a surgical gown, I transformed into someone else, like an actor emerging from behind the curtain. The work had to be done, but I had to separate from some part of myself in order to do it. It was as if I was watching myself with detachment, plunging the knife into dead flesh, slipping out the bloody organs, peeling away the layers of diseases, all alone in that deadly quiet morgue.

In a way, I should be thankful to old Charlie for forcing me to deal with the demon that had haunted me since I was six years old.

* * *

It was a warm summer day, and I was playing with elder sister Lan in the garden. A black monarch butterfly with yellow spots on its wings was flitting among the blossoms. I followed it around until it landed on a flower petal. I was about to pinch its wings between my fingers when the old housekeeper, Lin Ma, appeared on the veranda. "Come inside, little sisters!" she called out.

I pretended not to hear. I was too busy searching for the butterfly, which had just flown away. Lin Ma was determined to get us into the house. From the veranda, she shuffled down the stone steps on her little bound feet, grasping the railing for support. When she finally reached us in the garden, she was out of breath.

"Come in quickly! Your Ma is calling you!" I looked at Lin Ma's face, which now loomed above my own. Her eyes were wild, not at all like her usual self, and her voice made us obey. Quietly we followed her to our mother's room.

Ma was lying in bed, and Nai Nai, my maternal

grandmother, was sitting in a chair by her side. Dad was standing at the foot of the bed. We were led to the bedside opposite Nai Nai and I looked at Ma.

Ma was not seeing. Her eyes were closed. She waved her arms in the air and cried out:

"Help me! Somebody come help me! Save my life!" I thought she was trying to tease us, one of those make-believe plays.

"Lan! Lan! Save me! Save me!" Ma cried out. I looked at Lan for any clue of what was happening.

Nai Nai turned her tear-stricken face to Lan and said: "Answer your Ma! Say you are here! Say Ma, come back!"

Lan drew a deep breath and burst into tears. When she had gathered enough wind, she said in a small, trembling voice "Ma .... Come back .... Ma!"

I felt a sudden panic to see Lan cry. She was the leader of our clan, the one who was never afraid of anything. By then I realized Ma was not playing, and something was terribly wrong. I don't remember myself crying. I was thinking,"why doesn't she call my name? I could save her although I am not yet seven and Lan is eight."

By her bedside, Dad stood rigid, silent and stone-faced. I couldn't tell if he knew what was going on, but I knew his stomach was tied into a big knot, just like mine.

The next day, Ma was thrashing about in bed, moaning and muttering incomprehensible words. Two Taoist priests were summoned to the house. I peaked through a crack in the door to watch the strange goings-on. The priests were dressed in tall pointed caps and long flowing black gowns. In the hallway, they set up a large square table on which they placed gilded statues of gods, incense burners and candlesticks. For days, the priests burned incense and paper money and chanted incantations to invoke the spirits of heaven and earth. They prostrated themselves before the gods, and went into a trance. After lengthy communication with the world beyond, the priests came up with this insight.

On the fifth day of the fifth lunar month, the day of the Dragon Boat Festival, our family had gone on an outing aboard a houseboat moored along the banks of the Yangtze River. We watched the dragon boat race and had tea and *zengzi*, packets of sweet rice wrapped in bamboo leaves. It was an evil boat, the priests said, and a vicious murder had been committed there. As Ma walked on the deck, she had stepped on a dried bloodstain from the murdered man. That's how the ghost had attached itself to her body.

Lin Ma told me the world is full of ghosts of people who have died a violent death. These malicious ghosts are forever wandering in the wild, looking for substitutes. They like to haunt people whose *qi* is weakened by illness or sadness. The ghosts would go so far as to set traps to lure people to their deaths. Only when the ghost comes up with a substitute would the local earth god allow it to get on the Wheel of Incarnation so that it could be reborn again.

The night before Ma took sick, she went missing from her bed. When Dad and the servants went looking for her, they found her sitting under the moonlight by a well at the back of our house. The wooden cover of the well had been pushed aside. When they brought her back home, she had become incoherent and delirious.

I never for a moment questioned the adults' explanation of my mother's bizarre behavior. What would draw her to that well, the one which we had always been warned to stay away from, to perch on the edge so close to death? Why would she, a happy, loving mother, suddenly lose her mind? From my child's perspective, an angry ghost made as much sense as anything else did. The episode was so frightening, and so incomprehensible, it must have been a product of the supernatural. Nothing in our human world, I thought, could cause such anguish and pain.

The priests wasted no time getting on with the exorcism. They burned candles and incense and spent long hours chanting to the gods for intervention and help. They brandished their swords and performed *kung fu* to tame the ghost. They bribed the ghost with stacks of paper money and paper gold nuggets, which were placed in large sacks and burned. A miniature horse and carriage, constructed of colorful paper plastered over a willow frame, was set alight to allow the ghost to travel to the Wheel in comfort and style.

After a week of warfare with the ghost, the priests announced they had won. But Ma was still unconscious. The priests said her spirit was disconnected and wandering in the *yin* world, the world of ghosts and spirits. They attempted to summon Ma's spirit back by blowing on an ox horn, shiny from use. It gave a deep, drawn-out bleat like a wounded animal, so eerie it made my hair stand on end. The priests called out the name of my dead grandfather: "Hsia, old master, Hsia, old master, bring your daughter back." On a piece of coarse yellow paper, they wrote *fo*, cryptic sacred verse that has the power to bring back the spirit from beyond. They pierced the *fo* on the tip of a sword, set it on fire, collected the ashes in a bowl of water and presented to my mother to drink.

Two doctors, a Western-trained doctor and a traditional herbal medicine man, were called in to see Ma. The Western doctor gave pills and shots, and the Chinese doctor prescribed eight different packets of rare herbs to be brewed in a clay pot over a slow charcoal fire. The aroma of the Chinese herbal medicine permeated the house and so saturated my brain that in the years to come, a whiff of that herbal aroma would instantly send me reeling.

Slowly, Ma regained consciousness, but she had become a stranger to me. She had once been a joyful and sociable person, always busy with new projects for her children and family. Now she looked like a ghost herself, not smiling, not talking, not reading books to us, not doing anything. She would not leave her bed, and the servants had to bring food and ginseng tea to her. The ghost, I was told, had taken away my mother's *qi*, her life's vital force. She was never again the same.

Even after the Dragon Boat Ghost had been exorcized from our home, I was still afraid. "Where did the ghost go?" I began to wonder. "Now that the priests are gone, will it come back again and find a new substitute?" I looked everywhere for signs of the ghost, and was horrified to discover that it had found me and haunted me at night.

I began having recurrent nightmares.

Lan and I were huddled inside our family rickshaw. The top was down, the curtain tightly drawn, and it was pitch black all around. Our rickshaw puller, old Zhou, was running faster and faster. His feet slapped the ground and I could hear his panting. The rickshaw lurched violently on the bumpy road. We were running away from some nameless danger and I was terrified. I had the feeling that a ghastly man was chasing us, but I had no idea who he was or what he looked like.

The dream would end abruptly as I woke up, panting and sweating.

I was wracked with fear. I clung to Lan and at night begged her to accompany me to the toilet down the dimly-lit hallway. I was weak from lack of sleep, and I ate poorly. One day, I nearly fell down while going up a flight of steps. I sought out Lin Ma. "I am dizzy," I told her, "my head is spinning." She scolded me: "Children don't have spinning head."

When I started to lose weight, the adults said I needed a tonic. They brewed a bunch of herbs into a bowl of thick, dark liquid and forced me to drink it. The stuff tasted so bitter I spitted it out and clamped my mouth tight. It took two adults to hold me down and another person to pinch my nose so that I had to open my mouth to breathe. I coughed and gagged. Most of the medicine went to my lungs.

Nai Nai was the only adult to take notice of my sorry state of mind. To keep the ghost at bay, she produced an ancient copper coin with a square hole in the center. The coin was about two inches in diameter, much larger and thicker than the ones used as currency in ancient China. Four characters were inscribed on each side of the coin. On one side was written *tai shang lao jun* (venerable Lord Superior), and on the other side, *sha gui jiang jing* (killer of demons and ghosts). Nai Nai tied a red silk cord through the center hole and hung the coin around my neck. Red, the color of blood, is one of the few things that ghosts fear. I wore the coin for a while and was relieved to find my fear abating. Eventually I was able to pass through dark hallways by myself, half running. Then Nai Nai took the coin away, fearing its power might weaken my *qi*. As far as I can remember, I was the only child in my family who needed Nai Nai's magic coin to fend off a ghost.

No one ever mentioned the Dragon Boat Ghost again, as if it were just an incidental illness like mumps or chicken pox. It was not until I was a medical student when I made the connection between my mother's strange illness and her mental turmoil. It took me several more decades of soul searching to fully understand how the story behind the dragon boat ghost continued to haunt me as well.

Chapter 2

THREE-INCH GOLDEN LILY

I could not imagine what my childhood would have been like without the old folks, my maternal grandmother Hsia, who we called Nai Nai, and our housekeeper Lin Ma (Lin was her family name, Ma is short for Mama). They were stationed in the house like antique furniture before I came into this world. Like fire and water, the old ladies did not mix, yet their lives were tightly bound to each other by fate.

Nai Nai was born to a wealthy, scholarly family. As an only child, she was terribly spoiled. Her parents would boast that she was not only pretty and bright, but that her feet were the tiniest in the whole town. This was no small attribute at a time when the "three-inch golden lily" was considered the most desirable quality in a girl. Women were not encouraged to walk, and ladies were forbidden to go outside the main gate. On rare occasions when they did venture out, they were carried in sedan chairs on the shoulders of coolies. The curtains had to be drawn and their faces could not be seen. As a young girl, Nai Nai was taught the Chinese classics by a private tutor at home and mastered the kind of embroidery that was famous in the province.

I remembered Nai Nai as a lady of leisure. She had nothing in the world to do, so she passed her time sitting on top of her bed with an ancient Chinese water smoking pipe (a pipe connected to a palm-sized copper contraption that holds about one ounce of water), staring into space and brooding. Once in a while, she would take a puff from the pipe, or sigh and wipe tears off her face. After a long period of silence, she would find an excuse to start ranting and raving. She hated the weather, the places we lived, the food we ate and the people around her. The objects of her wrath were mostly the servants and the grandchildren.

"Bandits! You look like bandits!" she would shout at Lan and me. "Such coarse manners. No proper way to sit or stand." She obviously did not approve of our parents' way of raising children.

The only perfect person in the world was her youngest daughter, whom Nai Nai had not seen in years. Every day she cursed the Japanese for raising a war that had separated her from her favorite child.

Nai Nai had been thin and frail all her life. She was intolerant of the cold weather. A down quilt and a hot water bottle could not warm her bones during the cold winter nights. Because children were thought to generate *yang qi,* warm energy which counteracts the cold *yin qi* in the bodies of old people, Lan was assigned to sleep at the end of Nai Nai's bed. But Lan was a restless sleeper and would often kick Nai Nai. The whole household would then be awakened by Nai Nai's curses. So eventually, the honor of warming Nai Nai's bed was passed on to me. On the first night, Nai Nai yelled at me after I turned over in my sleep. Being an obedient child and very anxious to please, I willed myself to remain motionless, sleeping like a mummy with my arms folded across my chest. This is how I continue to sleep today.

Nai Nai's way with the servants was merciless. She would burst into a rage if a servant, usually Lin Ma, showed even the slightest sign of neglect or disrespect, if she was late in bringing tea or failed to prepare her meals according to her specifications. The scolding would end in tears, and accusations of treachery.

"You lazy slave dog!" Nai Nai would yell. "You have a black heart! Aren't you afraid you will be born a cow or a horse in your next life?"

"So I am a slave dog." Lin Ma would murmur, with lowered eyes and tight lips. Lin Ma never talked back, she knew her place. Nai Nai was like a cruel empress when she was angry or miserable, and she was impossible to please.

The only person in our family who could touch the soft spot in Nai Nai's heart was my sister Na, who is two years younger than I. Na was a quiet and withdrawn child whom no one paid any attention to except during her crying spells. Without warning, Na would suddenly burst into a rising and falling, rhythmic type of wailing: "Ah .... Ah .... Ah" pausing for breaths in between. Family members would describe her cry as a "ghost's howl" that would make the soul cringe and the flesh jump. If anyone tried to console her, she would cry even louder. Finally after what seemed like an eternity, the storm in her would gradually subside.

No one seemed to have any inkling as to Na's problem. Child psychology was unheard of. Lin Ma suggested that we hire a Taoist priest to exorcize the ghost that was bothering Na. The only person who understood what was going on was Nai Nai. She would, on occasion, take Na into her room and pacify her with a few words and some treats.

Na was a middle child, caught between two extroverted older sisters and two younger brothers who were our mother's favorites. When Na was born, she did not even have a name. My parents were disappointed with the arrival of another baby girl. They simply called her *san-er*, or third child. When she started school, her name was changed to Hsiang Na, which was close to her nickname. Hsiang or Xiang in modern pinyin, is our generation name and Na means grace. She did not get a flower name such as Lan (day lily) or Mei (plum blossom). That was just the beginning of years of neglect that made her a lonely and anti-social child, and her crying fits made her even less likable.

Decades later, Na became a professor of physics at a prestigious university in China and the most sociable among her siblings. She confided to me that as a child she was exploding with a rage she could not comprehend and a determination to succeed in life. She said Lan and I always ganged up on her, something I could never remember doing. "You were as thick as thieves, and made me feel like an outcast!" she told me. Her accusations stunned me. I felt like a terrible big sister.

Like most women of their generation, Nai Nai and Lin Ma both had bound feet. They shuffled about the house in constant discomfort. But since Nai Nai's feet were particularly small, she suffered more than Lin Ma did. Every night, Nai Nai sat on a low stool and soaked her feet in a basin of hot water. It was a disgusting sight. The feet looked like twisted, flesh-covered bones mounted at the end of stick-thin pale legs. The toes were bent and curled underneath the soles of the feet like a tightened fist. She had to apply a loose binding just to give some support to the feet. During warm weather, a fungal infection would invade the crevices between the toes and the soles of the feet. The skin became red and raw, and Nai Nai would complain of intense itching. She tried all sorts of remedies, both traditional Chinese medicine and Western medicine, but with little success.

One day, while we were swimming in the ocean, a rickshaw pulled up close and in it sat Nai Nai with a little wooden stool and an umbrella on her lap. Lan and I helped her out of the rickshaw, supporting her arms while other siblings carried the stool and the umbrella. At the water's edge, we helped Nai Nai ease onto the stool. Then she removed her socks and soaked her feet in the seawater. It was a cure some local friend had recommended. The waves splashed, the sand shifted under her tiny stool, and the wind blew her hair in all directions. With one child holding the umbrella over Nai Nai's head, the rest lined up in a semicircle, silently watching as Nai Nai struggled to keep herself balanced on the stool, cursing the pounding ocean waves.

The seawater treatment eventually did some good and I was relieved that Nai Nai did not have to try the other remedy suggested by her opium-den friend. This is what she was instructed to do: catch the smallest toad you can find, take it by one foot and wash it by swishing it around in a bowl of clean water, open your mouth wide and put the toad on top of your tongue with its head facing the throat, pinch the frog's foot, let it go and close your mouth. When the toad jumps into your throat, you swallow it whole.

At first, I thought the old ladies were born with deformed feet. When I was nine or ten, I heard Lin Ma ranting in the kitchen about God's punishment to women. To Lin Ma, the two curses of womanhood were foot binding and childbirth.

"How pitifully the girl cries!" exclaimed Lin Ma, her face distorted by the memories of her own ordeal. "She is only five or six years old, her feet are tender and soft, she tries to run away, but aunts and grandmother hold her down. Her mother takes a roll of white cloth and wraps it around her feet over and over again, so tight that the bones feel like breaking. She can't eat, can't sleep, she screams and cries and begs her mother to take it off. Mother cries too, but she has to harden her heart. If a mother's heart gets soft, the girl's life will be forever ruined. No man would want a girl with big feet and she will grow up to hate her mother. The life of an unmarried woman is not too bad as long as her father is alive and can afford to keep her. But when the father dies, her brother becomes her master, and she will have to suffer mistreatment and humiliation from the brother's wife. If the brothers do not want to keep her, then she has to work as a servant or end up as a beggar on the street with no one to care for her in old age."

That scenario always sent chills down my spine and made me feel lucky to have escaped this inhumane treatment. As I grew older, I learned that the ancient custom was a major focus of erotic attraction and a perverted sexual fetish. In the old days, men liked to view, grasp and fondle the tiny, pointed lily feet. The tottering gait of a bound-foot woman was considered a symbol of feminine fragility that was desired by men.

I never knew what Nai Nai felt about womanhood and marriage. She never mentioned my late grandfather's name, as though he had never existed.

One day when I was about ten, younger sister Na burst into my room; I was alone reading by my desk. With wild eyes, flushed cheeks and a crop of spiky short hair, Na whispered in my ear: "I just heard a secret from Lin Ma. Our grandfather was killed by execution!"

Seeing that I was dumbfounded, Na made a ferocious face and said in a triumphant, know-it-all voice, "off with the head, do you understand?" Immediately, images of the ghosts of executed men portrayed in novels flashed across my mind; a floating white figure clutching a severed head by the hair and whispering in a hoarse voice: "Give me back my life!" I felt goose bumps running down my arms.

I began to understand. Execution and "off with the head" are punishments for criminals. Could it be that Grandfather was a bad man and had committed a crime for which he was punished by law? Was this the reason why the grown-ups in my family avoided talking about him? It was a question that had periodically surged in my mind, but as children, we were taught not to ask too many questions. What little I knew about my grandparents' lives came through the grapevine from Lin Ma.

GRANDFATHER'S MICROSCOPE

My grandparents were married while still in their late teens. The marriage was arranged by their parents with the help of a marriage broker, who saw to it, as the saying goes, that the front gate on both sides matched in height and status. It was indeed a perfect match: both families were wealthy and socially prominent, the groom was scholarly and the bride beautiful. The children came early but at long intervals because Grandfather was away from home for years at a stretch. When he did come home, he spoke about the world in a language only the oldest daughter could understand. My grandparents never quarreled in front of the servants or the children, but often they were not on speaking terms, and that included the months preceding Grandfather's untimely death.

Nai Nai's boredom with life caused her to take up opium smoking which was a popular pastime, particularly among the rich. It was something to which Grandfather vehemently objected. "Foreigners use the poison to make us weak, so they can invade our country and rob us clean!" Lin Ma recalled my grandfather saying. But Nai Nai did not heed her husband's warnings.

"She was born rich and always had her way." Lin Ma would explain.

Although she was privileged, Nai Nai in fact led a miserable life. At the time of her husband's brutal murder, Nai Nai was not even forty. Her only son was still a child, so she had to depend instead on her son-in-law, my father. Sons-in-law were referred to as half-sons, and by tradition, were obliged to take care of their wife's parents.

Then came my mother's mental breakdown and the family was in a state of collapse. For Nai Nai, it was another terrible blow. There was no escaping, only opium could dull the pain.

Nai Nai's best friend was a pretty young woman who used to come to our house to smoke opium and play mahjong. The two would lie crosswise on a large bed with their heads propped up on a pile of pillows inhaling the thick white smoke in deep gulps. Through the cloud of pungent smoke, and reflected in the flickering light of the opium lamp, Nai Nai's face looked peaceful and contented. She reminded me of the statues of the Goddess Guanyin.

The opium not only pacified Nai Nai, it was a miracle cure! When we had a stomachache or diarrhea, Nai Nai would blow opium smoke into our mouths and tell us to swallow it. It worked like magic. Nai Nai began to think of herself as a healer of sorts. It gave her the excuse she needed to continue her extravagant habit.

Nai Nai had another magic trick. Whenever one of us children had a sports injury, she would pour rice liquor into a large porcelain bowl and light it with a match. She would thrust her hand into the bowl of fire and, with blue flames dancing around her hand, she would scoop out the liquor and quickly rub it over the sprained ankle or knee. Then she would wrap the wounded part with bandages. By the next day, the pain and swelling would be gone. Even though Nai Nai behaved like a dragon lady and rarely showed open affection, I knew she cared deeply for us.

Lin Ma grew up on a farm and married a laborer. Her husband died while she was in her early twenties, leaving her with a five-year-old son. Lin Ma left her son in the care of relatives and came to be a servant in the house of my great-grandparents when Nai Nai was still a teenager. Lin Ma supported her son with the meager wage she earned. On Nai Nai's wedding day, Lin Ma was carried in a plain palanquin at the back of the wedding procession, almost as part of the dowry. In her new master's house, she helped raise four Hsia children and went through "thick and thin" with the Hsia family.

Lin Ma enjoyed two decades of prosperity in the Hsia house before disaster struck. Grandfather died unexpectedly, the house was ransacked and the family fortune was lost. That was how Nai Nai, Lin Ma, my two aunts and one uncle came to live with my newlywed parents in the city. Lin Ma never again saw her son. Immediately, she began taking care of another generation of children, the Liu children.

In my mind, Lin Ma was more like a second grandmother than a servant. In the good old days before the war, Lin Ma did not have to do menial work but supervised the servants and saw to it that every family member was well cared for. During the war, when the number of servants under her dwindled, Lin Ma became the family cook. After school, I liked to help out in the kitchen, washing and peeling vegetables, while Lin Ma lorded over a crackling wood fire, telling scary stories.

Lin Ma said every river and lake had a dragon. The mightiest of all, the dragon king, lived at the bottom of Dongting Lake near our hometown in Hunan. The dragon king had armies of fish, shrimp and crab to protect his crystal palace. When the dragon got restless, he rose out of the water and flew through the sky to show his power. He danced with his weapons and the clanging and clashing made thunder and lightning in the sky. He drew the river water into his gigantic mouth and sprayed it to make rain. If the people displeased him, he would raise the tide and send water over the riverbanks. The flood would turn cities and farms into lakes and people would perish. These were not just fairytales to Lin Ma, she firmed believed them. Twice in her life, she had been caught in massive floods; both times she narrowly escaped by clinging to tree branches. Only a dragon king could possess such power. In the past, people had to throw live animals or even boys and girls into the river as sacrifices to appease the dragon king.

"If you waste food or tell a lie, the dragon king will strike you with thunderbolts!" Lin Ma would warn us. She told us to take time chewing food, for if we were to swallow a whole peanut or a fruit seed, a tree would grow on top of our heads. Although I had never seen anyone carrying a tree on top of her head, I still took her warning to heart.

Lin Ma had an amazing memory. Though illiterate, she kept in her head a precise lunar calendar. She could remember the festivals and the birthdays of all the gods and of every member of the family. Every few days, she would announce the birthday of one of her gods whose name no one had ever heard. On these occasions, she would be even more fastidious than usual, cleaning up every crumb in the house.

Lin Ma was a vegetarian and thought it a sin to kill animals. She said animals were human incarnations and they had feelings just like us. On the farm, she said, she had seen cattle kneeling down begging with tears in their eyes before they were taken out to be slaughtered.

What Lin Ma said about ghosts and dragon kings made more sense to me than what I was learning about foreign gods in Catholic school and in church. For many years when I was a girl, I observed the birthdays of Lin Ma's gods and became a vegetarian. Now, I only remember the birthday of the Sun God because it falls on the same day as mine. Sharing a birthday with the Sun God, according to Lin Ma, may account for my fiery temperament.

A lifetime of hard work had made Lin Ma an exceedingly hardy person. She was stoic, never got sick, and was almost insensitive to pain. At age sixty, she had all her teeth and she used them to break thread and yank nails. No matter how much work awaited her, she went about her chores in a slow and steady pace. No matter how hard life became, or how deprived she was, she never complained. No one had ever seen her cry.

Lin Ma was very thrifty. She would save her meager wage, and would periodically ask my mother to shop on her behalf. She had saved two large trunks full of cotton fabric and good clothes which she never wore. The jacket and the apron she wore daily were thick as quilts with patch on top of patch. Although she wore clothes fit for a beggar, she was always spotlessly clean with her hair neatly pulled back into a bun on the back of her head.

Lin Ma would be considered handsome by modern standards. She had high cheekbones, deep-set eyes, a high-bridged nose, and a wide mouth with thin lips. But these were typical features of a slave, according to my father who prized himself an expert face-reader. A woman of fortune must have a smooth moon face, narrow slanted eyes and a small plump cherry mouth.

At the time, the Chinese believed that a woman with a hard fate could squash her husband and cause him to die at a young age. Lin Ma had accepted her bad fate as a punishment from god. She believed that she was a bad person in a previous life and had cheated Nai Nai; now they had to even the score. But still, she told us, it's better to be born a woman with a hard fate than an animal. Horses and cattle labored until they were too old to work, then they were sold to the butchers to be killed and eaten. By being a kind and religious person, she was bargaining for a better chance in her next reincarnation.

"What would you want to be in your next life?" I asked Lin Ma one day. She frowned, thought hard for a moment, and mumbled something I could not make out.

At the time, I was sure Lin Ma had wished to be born a lady like Nai Nai or Mother. But she must have realized that neither of them led a happy life. Maybe Lin Ma wanted to be like me, going to school, running free and making choices.

Chapter 3

GOLDEN RICE BOWL

Some of my fondest memories of my childhood were of the times I spent with my Father. My sister Lan and I would eagerly await the days when we could accompany him to the theater to watch him perform on stage. Dad had acquired a taste for Peking opera while in college. He loved everything about it: the stories, the singing, the orchestral music, the make-up and costumes, and the graceful, theatrical movements. Lan and I would follow him backstage and watch him prepare for his performances. As he sat before a small mirror, a makeup artist would pull the skin of his forehead taut under a black mesh binder, so that his eyes appeared slanted. All of his familiar lines, creases and folds would disappear under a thin mask of white paste paint. Then an entirely new face would appear, warm with rouge on the cheeks and eyelids, and eyes outlined and sharply angled with black accents. Finally, he would balance himself atop high platform shoes, and slip on a flowing, wide-sleeved robe and matching cap. From our hiding place behind the curtain, Lan and I would admire his transformation, and we would think that our father had truly turned into a mythical figure from China's past.

Dad's favorite opera was called "The fourth son visits his mother." It was about a Han Chinese, the 4th son of a famous General, who was captured by a barbarian army. He hid his identity, changed his name, and married a barbarian princess. After many years living among the barbarians, he finally confessed his secret to his wife who then arranged for his return home to visit his mother. My father sang the lead role. He didn't have the greatest voice, but what he lacked he made up for in theatricality. I can still see him on stage, kneeling before his elderly mother, weeping and singing as he lamented the sorrow of his long absence from home. I was still too young to fully understand that all of it was make-believe, and my heart ached seeing my own father so distraught.

Dad's passion for opera rubbed off on all of us. At home, we learned to sing famous arias from records played on a Victrola. On Sundays when our parents went out, we would have tea parties and put on our own opera shows. We would set the stage on a brick bed in a spare room, and sit our younger siblings on rows of little chairs in front of the stage. We would put on our mother's silk gowns, and wrap our heads with silk scarves studded with chicken feathers and toothpicks. We would sing whatever songs we knew and make up the rest as we went along. By the time our parents came home, the house would be carefully restored to order, and we would look bored as if nothing had happened.

My father was the Chinese version of a renaissance man. When times were good, he would spare no expense indulging in his artistic interests. He took up photography, a rare hobby in those days, and spent a fortune on imported photographic equipment, including a large Kodak camera, fitted with all kinds of lenses, an enlarger and printing equipment. Lan and I were his favorite photographic subjects. I remember him bending over the camera with a black cloth over his head, directing us to turn this way, look that way. The exposure was pure guesswork and was done manually by lifting and closing the lens cover. Then he would spend long hours in his darkroom making the prints perfect. Several of the photographs he took of Lan and me won prizes at competitions sponsored by Kodak magazine.

My father was also a connoisseur of good food and wine. He was an enthusiastic consumer of all kinds of Chinese regional foods. He had a special fondness, though, for Beijing cuisine. It was a unique blend of northern Han, Moslem, Mongolian and imperial Manchu influences. He raved about the Beijing lamb, which were raised in the wilderness north of the Great Wall and brought in during the fall when the meat was at its best. Thin slices of the meat were dipped into boiling broth for a few seconds and eaten with a spicy sauce. For him, food and wine were the prelude to the much more important event, telling stories to his assembled family members. As the saying goes: "An ounce of yellow wine unlocks the talking box."

Father was one of those rare people who was always an optimist. Even during the darkest days, he would still maintain an unwavering belief that good luck would someday return. Like most Chinese, he was a firm believer in fate and in the art of face reading. He attributed my mother's misfortunes entirely to her own bad karma and the unlucky features in her face. Her forehead, he insisted, was too low and narrow, and that's why she had bad luck in her youth. She was not destined to be rich because money was rolling out of her large, upturned nostrils. She did have some good features though. Her long chin and long ear lobes predicted a long life. Looking at my father, no one would doubt that he had the kind of face the Chinese describe as *fu*. His face spoke of kindness, stamina and success. He had a square jaw, a wide mouth, a long upper lip, and long ear lobes. Despite a low and narrow forehead, his eyes were large and his eyebrows lifting.

His nose was straight, with a full round tip. He believed that this feature could compensate for the deficiency in his wife's face.

At that time of my life, my father was my one true hero. He was easily the most interesting, exciting, loving and optimistic person I knew. I believed in him and loved him unconditionally. Those feelings would be hard to reconcile with what was to happen later.

In the days before the war, my family led an opulent lifestyle. Our large clan lived in a stately compound, filled with beautiful Chinese and European furniture. A staff of cook, cleaners, nannies, an errand boy and a rickshaw puller took care of us. My mother dressed us in the latest styles, tailor-made and copied from the photographs in European fashion magazines. We were well fed and well entertained. Compared with the majority of our countrymen, we lived lives of incredible luxury.

All of it came about because my father had a very good job. He was an executive at the Maritime Customs Service, China's version of the Customs House. It was far from an ordinary government bureaucracy, though. The British had set up the Customs Service in the 19th century, during an era when Western powers were forcing China to open its doors to trade. Despite its somewhat dubious origins, it became one of the few truly modern institutions within the Chinese government.

The British had established a special college in Beijing to train staff for the Customs Service. The curriculum was equivalent to that of a liberal art's college with emphasis on world history, international trade and maritime law. Many of the professors were British. Upon graduation, students had their pick of jobs around the country. The salary scale was set by the British and was quite generous. It was a guaranteed, lifelong job with health and retirement benefits, what the Chinese called a "golden rice bowl."

My father was the only person in his hometown who was accepted by the college, but he did not have money to go to Beijing. By a streak of luck, one of his friends had won a lottery, and had tried to persuade my father to go to France with him to study Socialism. My father turned down the offer, but borrowed money to go to Beijing.

Graduates of the college were an elite group. They were intelligent young men who spoke Oxford English and were well informed on world affairs. They were expected to dress in fashionable Western clothing or naval uniforms. They were transferred to new posts every few years, in order to limit the opportunities for collusion with the locals. By and large, Customs people did not mix well with local populations who regarded them as transients. So the Customs people formed a tight-knit group, and looked out for one another.

By the time my father was in his late teens, he was already a married man with a child. According to old Chinese custom, Father was married at the age of sixteen to an older girl his parents had chosen for him. In his time, young boys were often betrothed to older girls who were expected to have a hand in raising their husbands. After the birth of his daughter Yu, meaning Jade, Father went off to college and was seldom home. Tragically, his wife died at a young age. But beyond that, I know nothing about her.

Father's marriage to my mother was an entirely different matter. He had known her for years, having once been a star pupil of her father's. My mother was from an intellectual family, and was the first woman in town to attend college in Shanghai, the most cosmopolitan of Chinese cities. There she studied economics and was exposed to western ideas. But then her privileged world suddenly collapsed due to the unexpected death of her father. My mother was the eldest child, and the responsibility for her mother and three younger siblings fell on her shoulders. She dropped out of school and the pressure was on to marry.

The townspeople praised the union as a good match. My father was a dutiful son-in-law. He invited my newly widowed grandmother Nai Nai, her three children, aged nine to fifteen, and the housekeeper Lin Ma to come live with him and his new wife. He not only supported his new extended family, but he sent all my mother's siblings to boarding schools. His daughter from his first marriage grew up with us as well.

After the wedding, the children arrived in quick succession. My mother gradually put aside her own ambitions to enjoy her new life as wife and mother. It was her job every day to plan the family menu and give instructions to the servants. Instead of studying economics, Mother kept up to date on issues of health, education, and fashion, and earned the nickname "foreign doctor" among the other housewives. She could speak a little English and would sometimes accompany my father to dinners in the private club frequented by my father's British colleagues. At that time, she was our small town's equivalent of a society lady.

We owned a handsome new rickshaw which was kept in a little shed in the back yard. Our rickshaw puller, old Zhou, was in his 30s' but looked much older with his sun-tanned, wrinkled skin. His eyes were perpetually inflamed and red. Unlike the self-employed rickshaw pullers who had to labor all day to earn the equivalent of a bowl or two of rice, old Zhou had a relatively soft job and considered himself lucky. His routine was to send Lan and me to and from school and the master to and from work each day. Mother sometimes took shopping trips in the rickshaw. Old Zhou had meals in our house with the other servants, and took home a few dollars each month along with our family's cast-off clothing for his three children.

In my memory, the rickshaw was as comfortable as a luxury automobile. On sunny days, Old Zhou would fold back the black oil-cloth top like a convertible. In bad weather, he would pull the top forward and draw a curtain in front to shield us from the wind and rain. In the winter, he would drape a woolen blanket over our laps. On the way to school in the morning, old Zhou would stop at a little teahouse and let us have our breakfast of steaming soybean milk and *you tiao*, deep-fried long donut strips.

It was Old Zhou who unintentionally spilled the beans about my father's deep dark secret. One day, my mother was on her way to the kitchen to give the cook some instructions. Old Zhou was sitting at the table with the other servants. "I am taking the master to *the little house*," he said, not knowing that my mother was within hearing distance. She froze at the door. Her initial suspicion which later turned out to be true, was any wife's worst fear.

I don't know if she interrogated the servants, or if she eventually confronted my father. But the truth was worse than she had imagined. The mistress that my father had kept for the previous six years, who had born him two children, was her own younger sister, Yuen, whom we called First Aunt.

The affair had begun only the year after my parents' marriage. First Aunt was practically a child, just 16 years old. When my mother gave birth to my eldest sister, Lan, she had serious postpartum complications. The affair had begun when my mother was struggling for her life in the hospital. Before long, First Aunt left for boarding school and we saw her only rarely.

Polygamy was a fact of life in old China, and legal as well. By custom, men were allowed to take as many wives as their hearts desired. In fact, multiple wives, like a bulging belly, was a symbol of a man's wealth and status. The first wife was expected to put up with the minor wives with civility and dignity. Some even went so far as to choose concubines for their husbands. In return for this unselfishness, the first wife maintained her status as the head of *the large house*, while the concubines belonged to *the little house*. The concubines were required by custom to be subservient to the first wife whom they addressed as "elder sister." If everyone played her card right, a harmonious hierarchical order was established and the lord of the household was considered fortunate and the object of envy. That was the ideal. Of course the reality was usually much different. Jealousy, intrigue and fights between the wives and children were facts of daily life.

My mother came from a progressive family, and as a university student she was indoctrinated with progressive ideas. She was a confirmed feminist, and she abhorred the practice of double standards and the subservience of women. To discover that the two persons she had trusted most in the world had betrayed her was devastating.

I can only guess my mother's reaction when she discovered the truth. I can only imagine how horrified she must have been. I now know that the discovery of the affair was the beginning of her mental deterioration, beginning with the awful experience of the Dragon Boat Ghost and ending with her death forty years later.

Once an optimistic and jolly person, my mother became morose and withdrawn. She would look out at the world with listless, non-comprehending eyes. There were days when she would not say a word. She became paranoid and could not bring herself to trust anyone. Her sinking spirit evidently affected her health. She was plagued by chronic bronchitis and asthmatic attacks. By the time she turned forty, she seemed like an old woman.

Mother never mentioned my father's affair and no one dared to ask her about it. Chinese children were taught to live in a sort of silence speaking only when necessary in the presence of adults. We kept our thoughts and secrets to ourselves. I was puzzled by many of the things that adults did, but never dared to criticize or question them. We had learned from Confucius to unconditionally obey authority. To question or disobey your elders was the greatest sin.

I came to hate my father and my aunt for having betrayed

my mother and injured her so severely. Since father-hating was not permitted in my culture, I took it out on my aunt and her children. I would provoke an argument or a fight, and the adults would intervene. It always seemed to me that my father would take their side. One day Nai Nai took me aside and tearfully scolded me.

"Your mother's health is not good. If you keep on making trouble for her, she may die." That remark put a damper on my aggressive behavior. I had come to understand why Nai Nai was always in a bad mood and what had driven her to opium. After the untimely death of her husband and the breakdown of her family, she had to live as a guest in her daughter's house. Now her own daughters were caught up in the disgrace, and were now rivals for one man's affection.

During the winter when I was twelve, my mother's bronchitis got the best of her. One evening, she was feverish, coughing, wheezing and struggling for breath. Nai Nai was at the bedside and I could read in her face that Mother was in serious danger. I was so distraught that I went to my room to try to think of a way to save her.

I remembered the legendary story of a girl who had saved her dying mother by cutting out a piece of her own flesh and cooking it into herbal medicine. The mother got well because God took pity and rewarded her filial devotion. Alone in my room, I took a pair of rusty scissors out of my drawer. Several times I put the cold metal against my arm, and then recoiled. I could not muster enough courage to cut my own flesh. In the end, I put down the scissors and cried out of shame for being a selfish coward. Luckily for me, she survived, even without my flesh.

Throughout my childhood, I often daydreamed that my father had never committed his awful mistake, so that he could remain in my heart as my true idol. In my darkest moments, I prayed to god to make *the little house* disappear. I even tried to make a deal with god that if I cut off a piece of my flesh, peace and harmony would return to my family. But it was not to be.

At the time, I had no idea what I wanted to be when I grew up, but I knew I did not want to be like my mother. She had also made it clear that she did not want me to be like her. On rare occasions when other siblings were out of sight, and I had a private moment with her, she would often say to me: "How nice it would be if you could be independent and have your own career. Men are not trustworthy!"

She would repeat this over and over again to each of her four daughters until it was deeply etched in our brains. Decades later, when my mother was long gone, my sisters and I would get together and recall the only sentence we remembered her saying: "You have to study hard, have your own career and eat whatever you like."

"Eat whatever you like" is a common Chinese saying, meaning to have total luxury and freedom. In a country where choices are limited, to be able to eat what you like means that you have control over your life. It was something few women ever achieved.

I believe what saved my mother's sanity was her mahjong games. Mahjong was to Mother what opium was to Nai Nai. Every few days, I would come home from school and find the living room alive with laughter and the clicking of mahjong tiles. I liked to stand behind Mother and watch her become alive. She would have this little smile on her face, and her hands would fly over the tiles. My mother had a quick and calculating mind, and she could keep track of all the tiles. She claimed that she could tell a lot about people's characters by the way they played mahjong. That's why some people were never invited back again. I could not remember a time when my mother lost a game. They had this rule: the loser's money, instead of going to the winner, would pay for the dinner that evening. Needless to say, our family had a lot of free meals.

My last mental image of my mother was of her sitting at the mahjong table. On that day, I was leaving home for medical school after the winter break. Father was taking me to the airport. I stopped at the door, turned and looked at Mother. Somehow I had a strange feeling that I might never see her again. I said: "Ma, I am going!"

She paused for a second, nodded, then continued playing mahjong. She didn't look up, or say a word. Perhaps she was having the same premonition as I did, but was too afraid to meet my eyes. That was the last time I saw my family.

Despite my parents' disastrous marriage, the two of them did have a common goal. They invested all their energy in the cultivation of their children, and for that I am grateful. Being an only child, my father wanted as many children as god would grant him. He had always claimed that his ten children were his only true achievement in life.

But the strain of sustaining a big family during wartime took its toll. My younger sisters and brothers did not get nearly as much attention as the two oldest ones did, and they were resentful. From an early age, my parents made sure that Lan and I understood the responsibility of our position within the family. As the eldest we were privileged, but we also had to help raise our younger siblings and to take care of our parents in their old age.

Our parents had progressive ideas about raising children. They did not want us to be the stereotypical "book worms" or "Asian invalids." Besides studying, they encouraged us to play, and to participate in sports, arts, music, drama and dance.

During the long summer vacations, we had to practice calligraphy under the watchful eye of our mother. She made sure that we held the brush in a straight upright position and that our wrists did not touch the desk. Each character had to be written in a precise sequence and strokes. During the years of Japanese occupation, English was banned in school, so

Father taught us English at home. The only English books we had were those from his college days: World History, Shakespeare and "The Arabian Nights." From the history book, I learned, for the first time, the gruesome details of the French and Russian revolutions. I was most impressed by the Shakespeare, an old volume with a grey hard cover. What struck me as unusual about the book were the hand-written Japanese characters on some pages. At the time, I was learning Japanese in school, but Father had never studied Japanese. I was puzzled, so I asked:

"Who wrote these Japanese characters?"

"Your grandfather," he replied.

I had wanted to hear more about my grandfather, but Father went ahead to read Hamlet.

Father also taught Lan and me the classical Chinese literature he had learned as a child. He would be transported to a dreamy world as he recited, in a peculiar Hunan sing-song style, his favorite essay, "Memoir of the Peach Blossom Valley" written by the celebrated poet and philosopher Tao Yuanming (born around AD 350). It was about a fisherman who chanced upon a utopian society hidden in a valley among peach blossom groves. (The present day Peach Blossom town is located fifty miles west of Dongting Lake near our hometown). The essay was a revelation of the author's inner life; he was a naturalist with Taoist views. His simple and concise narrative, as pure and smooth as pearls, had lent an air of profound beauty and mystery. To this day, I could still recite it word by word.

Of all the children, Lan was the one who had inherited our father's artistic talent to the fullest. A very mischievous child, she was always plotting strategies, inventing interesting games and dare devil acts. All we had to do was to follow her. She wrote a poem entitled "The Sea" when she was ten. It went something like this:

Big sea, my mother:
> The soft wind blowing on your sapphire waves,
> sparkling with golden drops of sunshine.
> I rock gently in your great bosom,
> as fish swim below.
> Blessed to have a mother like you.

Big sea, my mother:
> Gales gush in between water spray,
> waves tumbling from heaven,
> Fierce roar, darkening sky,
> I stand humbly by your side, awed by your might.
> Be gentle, be calm.
> Let me return to you.

Big sea, my mother.

At my parents' suggestion, Lan submitted the poem to the local newspaper under the pen name "Seagull." When the poem was published in the paper, the whole family was elated.

I had accepted Lan's superiority without question or jealousy. Who could blame my parents for favoring Lan? Besides being a fine writer, she could draw and paint. She was a good actor and a fine singer with a lovely soprano voice. She often performed on stage at school.

My parents recognized the genius in their first child and did their best to develop her potential. Mother arranged for Lan to take piano lessons with Miss Liu, the principle of our school and the only pianist in town. Lan also took drawing lessons from Mr. Li, an artist who owned a school-supply shop across the street from our school.

While Lan could write beautiful poems and impressive essays, my most dreaded subject was composition. I always felt I had nothing to say. While Lan was a natural artist, I was totally inept at drawing. I loved music and could sing fairly well, but no one knew I had a voice. My scholastic record was mediocre. I was regarded, by others as well as by myself, as an unremarkable child. Then came an incident that would change my life.

One day during an Algebra class, I was lost in a daydream. In those days, the object of my romantic dreams was my father's younger colleague Mr. Li, a tall and handsome young man with exquisite facial features. Father who had an eye for beauty, had taken a photographic portrait of Li and kept it in our family album. Father said Li had a rare kind of beauty and grace, combined with scholastic talent. The admiration was mutual, and Li was a frequent visitor in our house. As a rule, when my father had visitors, we children were kept out of the living room. I only caught glimpses of Mr. Li as he passed through the courtyard. His gait was light and elegant, like the Chinese saying, "floating like fairy."

During that fateful Algebra class, I didn't hear a word the teacher was saying. When it came time to do my homework, I was clueless. Finally I had to fabricate what seemed like a simple and logical formula to solve the equations. The following day, I was prepared for a good scolding for putting all that nonsense in my homework. But our teacher Mr. Su, a recent graduate of the renowned Qinghua University (China's MIT) in Beijing, said with an indulgent smile: "Follow the rules I told you when solving the equation. Don't invent your own rules even though you have come up with the right answer."

Upon graduation, Mr. Su wrote in my class memo book, a page of handsome calligraphy. It began with a short poem I no longer remember, followed by this personal message:

"Hsiang Mei, you have exceptional talent, wisdom, and

a distinctive grace. Study hard! Wherever you direct your will, you will soon succeed."

Those words etched deeply in my brain, and made a complete turnaround in my perception of myself. I no longer thought of myself as mediocre, and I set myself up to prove it. I gave up daydreaming and concentrated on my studies. The following year, I rose to the top of my class and stayed there. In the years to come, those wonderful words written in exuberant Chinese calligraphy had become my secret weapon. Whenever I was discouraged by failure and tortured by self-doubt, I would recall that calligraphy. It sustained me and restored my confidence during the darkest moments of my life.

That's how I came to be branded the scientist in the family, and it's a condition that eventually led me into medical school.

Studio portrait of Mei's parents taken in Weihai. Father was 41, Mother was 32. Circa 1940.

A prize-winning photograph taken by Father when Mei (left) was five and Lan (right) was six. Circa 1934.

A prize-winning photograph taken by Father of six-year-old Mei. Circa 1935.

Chapter 4

Hunan, my ancestral home

My mother said to me when I was twelve: "It is your ear lobe that saved your life." She was referring to an incident that occurred when I was six months old.

"We were staying in an inn," said my mother, "escaping disaster." The year was 1930. My family consisted of my parents, my two-year-old sister Lan and me. We were living in Changsha, the capital of Hunan province.

"One day, we took Lan downstairs to lunch and left you sleeping in bed. When we went back to our room, we bumped into a tea waiter on the stairway. He was rushing downstairs carrying you in his arms. When he saw us, he was flustered and said he heard you cry, so he picked you up and was bringing you to us in the dining room."

Mother narrowed her eyes and a look of fierce protectiveness appeared on her face.

"He was lying! He had his eye on you! You were white and plump, good for him to steal and sell." In those days, kidnapping was rampant, and there was a thriving market for children. Girls who were born plain would be sold as slaves. The pretty ones were not so lucky; they would be sold at higher prices into houses of prostitution where a life of misery, suffering and an early death awaited them. My mother said God had not meant for me to suffer such an unspeakable fate. I was born with long ear lobes, which denotes *fu*: good fortune and protection from disasters. As it turned out, these earlobes have served me well, both then and in the subsequent disasters that have plagued me.

My mother never told me, nor did I ask, what kind of disaster we were escaping. Disaster was to the Chinese a fact of life, something as common as thunder and lightening, and equally inexplicable. Disaster could be any of a number of things: war, uprising, flood, drought or famine. The Chinese have come to accept disaster as fate, without question or protest, and they adapt and survive. Chinese survivors are like cats; they have fast feet, good intuition and nine lives.

Much later in life when my parents were no longer there to answer my questions, I gathered, out of bits of remembered conversation and links in history books, that we were escaping the first onslaught of the Chinese civil war in our home province where so much turmoil began.

When a Chinese person wants to know something about another, he would ask, among other things, "where is your old home?" The name of your ancestral home, not your birth place, appears in all personal documents under *ji guan*, an equivalent of citizenship. Where your ancestors' bones are buried is thought to be the place where your soul is stored, and it says much about your character, your perception of yourself, and your place in history.

My old home is and always will be Hunan, and I will always be a Hunanese, even though I left the place when I was a toddler and went back for the first time only in my old age.

Hunan is located in south central China. It sits on the southern shore of an enormous body of inland water called Dongting lake (*hu* means lake, *nan* means south). Hubei province sits to the north of the lake (*bei* means north). With its fertile soil and abundant irrigation, Hunan is known as "fish and rice country," and an area that is prone to devastating floods. Four rivers meander through the province. The largest, the Hsiang River, flows into Dongting Lake and eventually connects with the Yangtze River. Hsiang or Xiang in modern pinyin, is a nickname for Hunan, and it is also my first name.

In ancient times, the twin lake states of Hunan and Hubei belonged to the kingdom of Zhu, the birthplace of a number of celebrated poets and philosophers: Laozi, Qu Yuan and Tao Yuanming among others. The lake was a great source of inspiration to them. Throughout history, the nearby mountains were hideouts for hermits, poets, rebels and bandits alike. Hunan people are known for their rebellious and stubborn temper, their daring spirit and a love of poetry. Many people think of them as the Chinese equivalent of the Irish. The men are fierce fighters, the women are known for their passion and they are all addicted to hot pepper.

In recent times, Mao Zedong was China's most famous Hunanese. The leader of the Communist Party was the son of a small landowner in Hunan. After graduating from high school, he went to Beijing, or Peking as it used to be called, and worked in the library of Peking University, where he was exposed to Marxist and Anarchist ideas that were being brought back by Chinese students returning from overseas. The chief proponent of Marxism was Li Dazhou, the head librarian who had just returned from Japan and who later founded the Chinese Communist Party. Mao returned to Hunan and began plotting anti-establishment activities. His movement turned to violence in 1927 when he organizing students, peasants and miners, and took up arms against the rich. Mao's army of 2,000 had twice attempted the "autumn harvest uprising" which was quickly put down by local militia and warlords aided by landowners who had suffered at the hands of the recent peasant uprising. Thousands of Communist members in the region were slaughtered.

I, among my siblings, was the one who had inherited a full measure of the Hunan spirit. My nickname was Thunderbolt. I was willful and stubborn, difficult for the adults to control. I remember the time when I was around three years old, they often threatened to have the "net lady" come and take me away.

The net lady came to the house regularly to sell hairnets, hairpins, combs and hair oil out of a bamboo basket carried in her hand. She was a middle-aged, thin and willowy woman with a sallow complexion. She wore a black Mandarin jacket and slacks with wide bottoms, and staggered and swayed on account of her small bound feet.

What frightened me most about this woman were her large, protruding eyes. The net lady would stare at me with those unblinking, bulging eyes and say in a high-pitched singsong voice: "Are you a good girl, little sister?" I would run for cover under the bed and bury my head in my arms. I felt like a rabbit about to be snatched away by a hawk.

The place under the bed was not only a safe haven for me, but also for my father's friend whose name I will never know.

One night when everyone in the household had already gone to bed, there came a light knock on the back door. My father opened the door a crack and peered into the darkness.

"Old brother, it's me!" a male voice whispered, "my life is in danger!"

This friend, who I later learned was a Communist, was being hunted all over the city by the Nationalist secret police. My father let him in, hid him under my bed and murmured a prayer to Guanyin, the goddess of mercy.

A short while later, there came footsteps and pounding on the front door. My father, in his underclothes, peered through the crack in the door and found three young men dressed in street clothes. The men shouted: "Open the door, we are police detectives!"

My father let the men in and answered some questions. Then the detectives started to search the house. I saw shadows of human figures moving across the walls of my bedroom and the bright beams of flashlights darting into the dark corners and under the beds. At the time electricity had not come into use, and the rooms in our house were dimly lit by lanterns.

The entire household was awakened, but no one made a sound. Nai Nai started wringing her hands and wiping away tears.

After a while, the detectives went away. They found nothing.

My mother, who was well into her fourth pregnancy, heaved a deep sigh and collapsed on a chair. Had the police discovered the man, they surely would have taken my father and executed him as well.

My parents told the story many years later. "Ay-yah, so much blood shed, so many talented young people killed for nothing." Their voices cracked in the retelling; many of the dead were friends and schoolmates. "Just imagine, an army of defiant young men with hands tied and carrying their own name stakes behind their backs. As they marched to the execution ground, they shouted to the crowd lining the streets: 'Long live Communism!'"

The ruling Nationalists and the Communists had been allies during early 1920s. They had the common goals of fighting the imperialist enemies and building a strong and unified China. After the death in 1925 of Dr. Sun Yet-sen, founding father of the Republic, power was passed to his successor Chiang Kai-shek who had just returned from military training in the Soviet Union. Chiang was appointed director of the newly established Whampoa Military Academy in Guandong province. Chou Enlai who had just returned from France, became director of political information in the academy.

GRANDFATHER'S MICROSCOPE

At the time, China was in total chaos; the country was torn apart by warlords. In 1926, the Nationalists joined the Communists and their Soviet advisors and worked out a brilliant plan to reunify China. They organized an army and appointed Chiang Kai-shek as the Commander-in-Chief. From Guangdong, the Revolutionary army launched its famous "Northern Expedition," a three-prong advance pointing towards the northern cities of Beijing and Tianjin. The army started out with 100,000 men including the newly trained Whampoa cadets. The Communists, who did not have military power, moved ahead of the troops and organized local workers and peasants to transport military equipment and disrupt enemy lines. They also engaged in propaganda, staged uprisings in Shanghai and Wuhan and created social upheaval.

By a combination of fighting and political maneuvering, the Revolutionary army had achieved a stunning victory. In just two years, they had fulfilled Sun Yat-sen's dying wish of unification of China. Nanjing (meaning southern capital) was officially named capital of the Republic of China. The city of Beijing, meaning northern capital, was renamed Beiping, northern peace. The Nationalist-Communist alliance had sparkled a new spirit of nationalism, and optimism was in the air.

But deepening ideological differences and the struggle for dominance which began even before the launching of the Northern Expedition, quickly turned into fatal conflicts. After brief attempts to reconcile, the Nationalists declared open war, and everywhere Communists were arrested and executed. In 1927, Li Dazhao, co-founder of the Chinese Communist Party was arrested and hanged by the powerful warlord general Zhang Zuoling from Manchuria.

In this era of shifting political alliances, my father managed to toe the line. He was a progressive-minded intellectual, and many of his closest friends were devout Marxists. But he never revealed his own political sympathies. It was dangerous to have any connection with Communists during the time we lived under Nationalist rule.

From early on, my parents must have decided to keep us children out of the complicated and dangerous business of politics. They never talked to us about the earth-shaking events that were going on around us. Whatever I know about the politics of the time, I gleaned from reading history books when I was well into my middle age and living in America.

So now I wonder: how had the man under my bed escaped police detection that night? Was it really the Guanyin goddess or the ghost of my grandfather who had blinded the detectives' eyes? Or had the sight of a pregnant wife and young children brought out the humanity in their hearts? Or could it be that one of them was actually a counterspy? I also wonder who was the man under my bed? Did he die anonymously or live to become a prominent member of the Communist party?

Sometimes I would torture myself with this question: "What would have happened to us all if they had taken my father away that night?" There were so many people depending on him for survival: his wives and children, parents and relatives on both his and my mother's sides. If he were imprisoned or killed, all of us would become beggars on the street. He had taken an awful risk! But then it was not in his nature to turn down a friend in need.

My father was the most generous person I know. Over the years, our guestroom housed a constant stream of needy friends and poor relations.

"They came to the city looking for jobs." Mother recalled years later. "They only had shabby clothes on their backs and I had to buy them new clothes and bedding. But how could they find a job? *bo wen bo wu* (can't write, can't fight). After a few months, we sent them home with money in the pocket. Next year, they were back again; the money was gone and so were the new clothes and bedding. We had to start all over again."

Father seemed embarrassed, "*how la*, oh well, we can afford to help them."

I had never heard him criticize or belittle anyone, especially people who were down and out on their luck. He was like a defense lawyer, forever finding excuses for people who had failed in life. He was always willing to help at the cost of personal loss and danger. These were personality traits that I consider heroic and admirable. But then again, the Hunan people are big on *yie*, loyalty and fair play.

In 1936 when I was seven, my father was transferred north and all ties with our hometown were severed. We left behind that dangerous cauldron of political dissent. But it wasn't long before we were caught in the upheaval again.

Chapter 5

SONG GIRL'S IGNORANCE

In 1936, our family moved to the city of Weihai (formerly Weihaiwei), which means "Glorious Sea Fortress" on the northern coast of Shandong province. For our family, which was deeply rooted in the inland south, it was like going to a foreign country. Everything was different: the weather, the landscape, the dialect, the customs and the food. The old ladies hated it the minute they set their little feet on the ground. But they thought the stay would be temporary. At the time, no one knew that the Sino-Japanese war was to break out in a year's time, leaving us stranded for ten long years.

Shandong was a sparsely populated, rural province. With the Yellow River running on its northern border, it was the cradle of Chinese civilization and the birth place of two great sages, Confucius and Mencius. The Shandong people tend to be taller and stronger than southerners. They are well known for their honesty, generosity and steadfastness.

When we lived in Weihai, our lives were simple and tranquil. The only excitement took place at the Catholic school, which was run by strange-looking women covered from head to toe with long black outfits with only their pale faces showing. They spoke Chinese in a funny way. Years before, a Catholic order had established this large complex consisting of a church, a boys' school, a girls' school and a handicraft factory. The boys' school was named "Sea Star Primary School" and the girls' school "Bright Star Primary School." I do not remember the nuns' nationality, but it made no difference to us anyhow. They were all *yang gui zi*, (foreign devil or ghost), which, by the way, is not an altogether disrespectful term.

I remember the first time I ever saw a Catholic Mass. The girls gathered at a small chapel at the back of the school. We sat mystified as the priests, in their strange costume, performed a variety of incomprehensible rituals at the altar. I remember being fascinated by the statues of the foreign gods, which were so different from our own. The organ music was beautiful and gave me a feeling of mystery and tranquility that I had not experienced before.

One day, in a fit of religious passion, I went across the street to Mr. Li's Bookstore and bought a little pocket Bible and a rosary. From then on, I attended mass with enthusiasm, even though I still had no idea what the chants and the Bible were all about.

My mother, who had gone to a missionary college in Shanghai, was quite pleased with our exposure to Western civilization. As Christianity began to take hold in our town, my mother became a believer. She sometimes took us to attend church services on Sundays. My father, on the other hand, was a Buddhist, but this created no conflict in the family. The Chinese tend to be very open-minded about religion. Perhaps that's because they don't really know what to believe. To begin with, they have a host of indigenous gods and saints, that vary in each locale. Then came Buddhism from India, Islam from the Middle East, and Christianity from the West. All of these foreign religions, particularly Buddhism, gained adherents among the pragmatic Chinese. I once heard an old lady, when asked about her religion, reply with enthusiasm:

"I believe in them all, Buddhist, Taoist, Christian, Catholic. After all, you want to have more than one son." She was one wise lady who did not want to take a chance.

One Sunday afternoon, a preacher from Mother's church came to our house and tried to convert my father. I eavesdropped and heard my father ask the preacher a question: "According to your belief, where did Master Confucius go, Heaven or Hell?"

"Oh, he is in Hell," the priest responded without hesitation, "because he did not believe in Christ and his sins were not forgiven."

"Well, I will be honored to be with Confucius one day." My father's blasphemy drove the preacher away.

Family picture taken in the court yard of the family home in Weihai at the beginning of the Sino-Japanese war when Mei was about ten. Front row, left to right: Yijien, Yisheng, Yiwu (half-brother). Back row, left to right: Na, Mei, Mother, Nai Nai, First Aunt, Lan, Lian (half sister). Circa 1938. Photograph by Father.

During our second summer in Weihai, dark clouds were gathering overhead. My father, who had always been a jolly person, suddenly became sullen and preoccupied. When he came home from work, he would hurry to his room, close the door and listen to the short-wave radio. The mood in the town changed as well. People began to stay home and bolt their doors, and the streets were often deserted. Memories of the first Sino-Japanese war which took place in this very town were still fresh in their minds. (See addendum at end of chapter)

Late one night, we heard the sounds of soldiers marching in the streets. We thought they were preparing to defend the town. When no fighting materialized, we cautiously opened our doors the next morning and looked out onto the streets. We were shocked to see columns of strange-looking soldiers carrying shiny new weapons. At the head of the column was a large banner with a rising sun and the words "The Great Imperial Japan" written in *hanzi* (Chinese characters). The footsteps that we had heard the night before were our own soldiers retreating from town. The Japanese army had walked in, without a fight.

We were just kids, and the sight of the victorious army both frightened and thrilled us. The Japanese soldiers were short and sturdy, and looked sharp in their new tailored uniforms and leather boots. Although they had similar facial features, they stood in sharp contrast to the malnourished, ragtag Chinese soldiers we were used to seeing in our town. We heard through the grapevine that some of our troops had retreated to the south to regroup, while others had gone to the countryside to organize guerilla forces to fight the "devils" or "short bandits" as the Japanese were nicknamed.

The Japanese replaced the top officials in town with appointees of their puppet regime in Beijing. The new police force declared the possession of short-wave radios illegal. After my father was forced to turn in his radio, his only source of news was by word of mouth at the office. Each day, he sank more deeply into depression. After returning from the office, he would drop into his favorite chair, just sighing and not saying a word. Meanwhile, the newspapers run by the puppet regime applauded Japanese military victories in Shanghai and Nanjing. Our hometown had become a savage battleground, and we lost touch with all of our relatives there.

From my perspective as a schoolgirl, though, very little about our lives had changed. It seemed to me that it was business as usual, and that the residents in the town quietly accepted their fate. In school, our teachers no longer talked about patriotism, one of their favorite topics before the occupation. Certain segments of the history books were altered, and now made reference to the Japanese as the masterminds of the "Greater Asian Co-Prosperity Sphere." Every so often, the students were lined up and taken to the pier to welcome arriving Japanese officials. We waved Japanese flags and called out in unison: "Long live the Great Imperial Japan!"

We got a new school superintendent and a Japanese language teacher. Both were natives of Manchuria, which had long been under Japanese rule. They made the study of Japanese mandatory for students above the Fourth grade. This was our first exposure to Japanese language and culture. Some of the students started to sing popular Japanese songs. My sister Lan and I quickly learned the new tunes. One day, while I was singing one of these songs to myself at home, my father burst into the room.

"You are just like the song girls knowing not the grief of conquered land!" he roared, his face livid with rage.

My father was quoting from the poem "Mooring on the River Qinhuai" by the famous poet Du Mu of the Tang dynasty (A.D. 803-852).

> Cold water veiled in mist and shores steeped in moonlight
> I moor on the River Qinhuai near wine shops at night
> Where song girls knowing not the grief of conquered land
> Are singing songs composed by a captive ruler's hand
>
> (Translated by Xu Yuan-Zhong, in "300 Tang poems, a new translation," The Commercial Press, Hong Kong)

After that episode, I dared not study Japanese books or sing Japanese songs at home. I felt for the first time that there was a whole world of humiliation and pain that my schoolgirl's imagination could not begin to grasp. The realization was so profound, that even now, fifty years later, whenever I hear a Japanese song, I remember my father citing that poem, and I feel those same twinges of shame.

As far as the occupation was concerned, the Japanese would leave people alone unless they had participated in openly subversive activities or voiced anti-Japanese sentiments. The Japanese soldiers in the city were generally well-behaved. We heard stories of soldiers beating or kicking Chinese civilians, but we never saw such a thing ourselves.

By that time, the Japanese had occupied a large part of the country, and their forces were thinly spread. The best troops were out on the front lines fighting the Chinese Nationalist army. Only small numbers of soldiers were left to guard the cities they had already conquered. So the Japanese relied heavily on Chinese collaborators to administer their occupied territories. They were for the most part former Nationalist soldiers who had surrendered to the Japanese. These traitors were called "dogs" or "second devils" by their fellow countrymen. But the civilians still preferred to deal with the dogs rather than the devils; at least they shared the same culture and language. The dogs thus served as a buffer between the conquerors and the conquered. We later learned that many of these collaborators were actually double agents, serving as spies for either the Nationalists or the Communists, a fact which did much to clear their tarnished reputations.

While the Japanese were consolidating their control over the key cities, the countryside was being run by a mixture of Nationalist and Communist guerrillas. At the beginning of the war with Japan, both parties had pledged to stop the civil war and to unite against the common enemy. In the years following the cease fire, the Communist force, designated the 8th Route Army, was able to build widespread grassroots support.

In those days, the Red Army had the reputation of being the most disciplined and well-behaved army in Chinese history. They fashioned themselves as "the People's soldiers." Instead of exploiting and terrorizing the villagers, the Communists behaved like sons and relatives. They worked side by side with the peasants in the field and helped the elderly carry water from the wells. They addressed the villagers as aunts, uncles and grandma.

While the Communists were gaining in popularity and morale, the Nationalist guerillas were increasingly marginalized. Power struggles and skirmishes led to formal battles. Once again the civil war intensified, and instead of fighting the Japanese, each sought to expand its own power base in preparation for the day of the Japanese defeat. By the end of the Second World War, the 8th Route Army had control over more than three quarters of Shandong province.

The communist guerillas had to rely on the farmers for food and on their enemies for ammunition. Hiding among the villagers, the Communists would stage daring raids on the Japanese forces whenever they ventured into the countryside. But the Japanese did not let such actions go unpunished. Together with their collaborators, they would mount a "clean sweep campaign" on any village that was suspected of giving refuge to Communists. In some instances, the Japanese would kill every living person in sight. Most of the time, however, the villagers were warned ahead of time by their intelligence sources. By the time the Japanese arrived, the residents had already dispersed into the woods and hills. The Japanese would then destroy whatever they could, killing the livestock and burning the village to the ground.

My younger brother heard a tale from a schoolmate who had relatives in the countryside. During a trip to a neighboring town, one of his relatives had come upon a deserted village where fighting had recently taken place. He peeked into someone's backyard and nearly died of fright. Mushrooming out of the ground like watermelons were human heads, with eyes and tongues popping out and blood running out of the orifices. Apparently the prisoners had been forced to dig a deep hole in the ground. They were then made to stand in the hole, as the dirt was shoveled back in. When the dirt reached the belly level, breathing became difficult and the blood could only pump to the head. When the dirt reached the chest level, the blood could not return to the heart which continued to pump blood to the head. The head would pulsate and expand like a purple balloon, and the prisoner would die an excruciating death. No one dared to say who had committed these atrocities.

We were living in a double world. On the surface, things were calm and in order, and nobody complained. But the terror was just beneath the surface.

After graduating from the Catholic primary school, Lan and I went to a newly-opened public middle school for girls in the old town district. It was in a dilapidated building that was the *yamen* or courthouse, during the Qing Dynasty. The class rooms and teachers' offices were located in a new wing in the front. The old buildings had inquisition halls with stone floors and high wooden beamed ceilings where swallows had built their nests. The only furnishings were two ping-pong tables. During recess, the halls reverberated with the sound of bouncing ping-pong balls and sweet girlish laughter.

Lan and I each got a second-hand bicycle for riding the mile to school. There were virtually no cars on the road, only an occasional horse-drawn carriage and rickshaw. Soon we were joined by a fifteen-year-old girl, Liu Ming, who lived up the hill from our house. All heads turned as the three Liu girls sped through the streets on their shiny bicycles. We were taken as sisters. Ming was a beautiful girl, taller and more mature than other girls of her age. She was an only child, and her mother took pride in dressing her in fashionable clothes. She was the only girl in our school who wore face powder and rouge. Ming was smart, worldly and stood out like a rose in bloom.

I really liked Ming because of her sweet and gentle disposition, and I wished she were my real sister. Ming treated me as the younger sister she never had.

One day Lan took me aside and, in an agitated manner, told me a rumor she had heard in school. Ming's father, who used to be a high government official, had now fallen on hard times. In order to make a living and to satisfy the father's opium habit, the rumor went, Ming's mother entertained Japanese soldiers at home. They said that Ming was an adopted child and was made into a prostitute to cater to the Japanese. I was horrified to hear this and refused to believe it at first. But as time went by, I became suspicious. Ming's Japanese was much better than anyone else's, and she was the one who circulated those Japanese songs.

As the rumors flew, our fellow students warned us that our association with Ming might tarnish our reputation. We finally succumbed to peer pressure and made some clumsy excuses not to ride with Ming to school. Ming soon caught on and went her own way. She became totally isolated and soon dropped out of school.

Not long afterwards, I heard that Ming was gravely ill. She had developed some sores in her nose which were spreading rapidly to her entire face. As I recalled, on several previous occasions, Ming had to keep a cotton plug in her nose because of nosebleeds. Rumor had it that she had syphilis. The disease rapidly spread to her brain and Ming died a terrible death.

On the day of Ming's funeral, the school sent representatives to her house with flowers. They said that Ming's face was horrible to see. Many students went to pay their condolences to her mother, but Lan and I did not go. I felt terribly ashamed for having abandoned Ming and having injured her feelings. It was a guilt that I carried all my life.

Decades later, after I became a doctor, I realized what had killed Ming was probably a malignant nasopharyngeal tumor. They were not the symptoms of syphilis, or any other sexually transmitted disease. On that front, the rumors were wrong. It made me wonder what other rumors were wrong as well.

After graduating from middle school, the highest place of learning in town, my parents decided to send Lan and me to a public high school in Yantai, or Smoke Port, sixty miles to the west. At the age of fifteen, I felt ready to fly out of the nest, but my parents feared that we might not be able to withstand the hardships of boarding school. Everyday, Mother drilled us on the rules of proper behavior: keep warm and clean, don't eat anything from street vendors, study hard, obey the teachers and write home often.

The distance from Weihai to Yantai was only sixty miles, but no car or bus dared run the route, for fear of getting caught in a guerilla ambush. The only way to get to Yantai was on the commercial boats which skirted the shore. The boats took all day to get there.

The high school had six classes, from 7th[th] to 12th grades. Each class had no more than thirty students. Most of the students were locals and lived at home, and the twenty or so boarders were distributed in two large bedrooms. The beds, made up of two wooden planks placed on top of two benches, were lined up against the walls. There were no bureaus or desks, so we kept our clothes in trunks under our beds. The superintendent, who was also our Chinese teacher, was a tiny young woman, a recent graduate of the prestigious Yenjing University in Beijing. She ruled with an iron fist, and made us adhere to a strict schedule. It was up at six, followed by morning study, breakfast at seven, group exercise at 7.45, and class at eight. Before supper at 5.30pm, we had an hour's free time to play basketball or to do some chores. When the bell rang at 6.30pm, everyone had to carry her books to the study room where the superintendent presided at the head table. We did our homework quietly, and no conversation was allowed until 8.30pm. Just before 9:00pm, the superintendent came to the rooms to check if everyone was in bed. At 9:00pm, the lights were turned out. Since the superintendent slept in the next room, we could not do anything except whisper. We were not allowed to go outside of the school except on Sundays.

We were totally unprepared for the kind of food served in the school. The morning meal consisted of millet gruel and rock-hard steamed bread made of moldy cornmeal. The side dishes were tasteless green vegetables, and we did not see meat or eggs for months on end. The worst kind of bread was that made of *gaoliang*, or red sorghum. It had a strange taste and caused severe constipation. Normally, *gaoliang* was used only as animal feed, but in hard times it sustained human lives in more than one way. The tall and dense *gaoliang* plants on the farm were favorite hiding places for guerillas.

The bad food and harsh living conditions made us terribly homesick. We lived in anticipation of letters and relief packages from home that contained delicate white bread, roasted peanuts, pickled fish and salted eggs. These packages were sent on board the steamers that ran twice weekly between Weihai and Yantai. When the ships were due into port, I would stand on the second floor balcony and watch the ships slowly emerge over the horizon. Our roommates were from rich farming families, and they would receive even more generous packages. We wrapped the food in paper and kept it under our beds.

Someone noticed that the food was disappearing. This caused some suspicion and finger pointing. One day, a girl returning to the dormitory at an unexpected hour caught the thief red-handed. It was a huge striped tomcat. The idea of having our precious food stolen from right under our noses was so infuriating that the girls decided to do away with the cat. They closed the door, cornered the cat and after a fierce struggle caught him. Then they carried him to the second floor balcony, the highest point in the building, and tossed him over. The cat did a mid-air somersault, then landed softly on the concrete and disappeared like lightening. We never saw him again.

My father had asked a colleague of his, Mr. Shi, to be our guardian. Mr. Shi lived near the school, and about once in a month, one of the Shi's six children would come by to invite us to a feast of dumplings stuffed with minced pork. I still remember how delicious those treats were and how they sustained our health and lifted our spirits.

Life in the boarding school was dreadfully boring. There was no radio or newspaper. We had no idea what was going on in the outside world. For tomboys like Lan and me, it was like living in a prison. The only positive aspect was that we were forced to concentrate on our studies. As a result, Lan and I both became top students, and we were competing with each other for the number one place in our class.

Spring finally arrived, and I was thrilled by the feel of warm sunlight and the fresh smell of spring air. One day after school, while standing on the second floor balcony and looking at the rolling ocean waves, I was overcome with an urge to walk on the beach and feel the wet sand under my feet. After talking with Lan and elder sister Chen, our roommate and good friend, we decided we were entitled to a break.

I went and told the superintendent that I had a bad toothache and that Lan and Chen were to accompany me to the dentist. Like birds out of a cage, we flew straight to a place called the "Jade Emperor's Peak," where spectacular rock formations dropped precipitously to the ocean. We climbed down the rocks, took off our shoes and socks, and jumped from one rock to another. I was shrieking gleefully like a seagull.

Then an unexpected thing happened. I lost my footing on a slippery rock and fell into the water. The underside of my left foot was cut by the rock's sharp edge. There was a stabbing pain followed by a gush of blood that would not stop. The girls tied my foot with stockings, but blood continued to ooze through it. With one girl holding my arm on each side, we climbed back up to the road at the top of the peak. Luckily a horse-drawn carriage happened to pass by, we all piled in and went back to school. The doctor was not in, so the superintendent washed and bandaged my wound. With a sarcastic smile, she remarked: "So you went to the dentist and got a nasty cut on your foot!"

At the end of the first year, we returned home for a long summer break. From my parents' constantly worried looks, I knew the war was getting worse. Rice and white flour were scarce. Meat and eggs were luxury items. The family had added corn meal, sweet potatoes and squash to our daily diet. People on the street generally looked hungry and listless. There were rumors that hundreds of people were dying of hunger each day on the streets of Shanghai. My parents were debating whether they could afford to send Lan and me back to boarding school, but finally they decided to give it another try.

Shortly after we went back to school for our second year, Lan came down with a bad case of diarrhea and abdominal pain that would not go away. The school doctor sent her stool sample to the public health laboratory and found out that she had bacillary dysentery. It remained a mystery as to how Lan had contracted the disease. We were eating the same drab, but thoroughly cooked food in school, and no one else was sick. The Japanese health authorities were fanatical about sanitation. Anyone found to have a communicable disease would be placed in isolation in the hospital until they were recovered which was rare or dead. The bodies were then cremated.

The hospital provided Lan with a clean, spacious room with two cots separated by a night stand. A chamber pot stood on the floor at one corner, and a wash basin filled with Lysol solution sat on a small stand in another corner. A Japanese nurse came each morning to take her pulse and temperature, but Lan never saw a doctor. The Japanese medical staff would not touch a Chinese patient, so the actual patient care was up to the family. I became Lan's private nurse.

Three times a day I went to the kitchen with two porcelain bowls to fetch meals for Lan. The cook would pour a thin rice gruel into one bowl and miso soup into another, making sure that her utensil did not touch the bowls. Three times a day, I put concentrated Lysol into the chamber pot, waited fifteen minutes, then carried it to the cesspool, dumped it and rinsed it several times with clean water. Afterwards, I soaked my hands in the basin of disinfectant. Between the hospital chores, I ran back and forth to school for classes and meals. After supper at school, I returned to the hospital, did my homework and slept on the cot opposite Lan. Fortunately the hospital was not far from the school.

After a week, Lan's condition was getting worse. She was having frequent cramps and ten to twenty small stools of white mucus mixed with blood. She was not getting any kind of medication, and the hospital food was barely keeping her alive. She was so weak she could hardly get out of bed. Since Lan had gotten sick, I hadn't heard from my parents because it took at least two weeks for letters to go back and forth. Long distance telephone was unheard of, and I didn't want to alarm my parents by sending a telegram.

One morning, the young Japanese nurse who came to check on Lan had a concerned look on her face. I took another look at Lan and saw a sinister sight. Her face was ashen, her large eyes were sunken and listless, and her skin was hanging loose over her bones. For the first time in my life, I realized I was looking at death in the face. I decided that something had to be done to save Lan's life.

I went to school and had a talk with the superintendent and the school doctor. I told them that Lan surely would die without medicine and asked the doctor if there was anything at all he could do. The doctor replied: "Yes, there is a new medicine on the market that is specific for bacillary dysentery, but it's very costly." I don't recall the exact amount, but it would take all the cash we had, money needed to see us through the semester. At first, I thought it sounded like a sales pitch, but then I didn't think the doctor dared to lie in front of the superintendent. Besides, I had no choice but to give it a try. So I gave him the money.

That evening, the doctor showed up in the hospital room with twelve little white pills. He told Lan to take two right away. As Lan was about to put the tablets into her mouth, she heard the price. Her hand dropped and she asked the doctor: "Do you guarantee it will work?"

"Just take it!" I yelled at her. She could not see herself as I had; there was no mirror in that room.

The following morning, the diarrhea and abdominal cramps stopped, and Lan was on her way to a swift recovery, much to the surprise of the doctors and nurses. They had given her up for dead. In retrospect, the tablets must have been a sulfa drug which was invented in the U.S. in 1936 and appeared on the black market in China during the early 40s. For all we knew, what had saved Lan's life could have been stolen goods from the Japanese military!

A few days later, I got a letter from home saying that our mother was preparing to come to Yantai to see Lan. I wired back saying that Lan was well and there was no need to come. The day Lan was discharged from the hospital, the nurses thoroughly drenched her and all her belongings with a disinfectant spay.

Returning to the dormitory, we received a large relief package from home. It was just what Lan needed. Her digestive system simply could not tolerate the coarse stuff served at the school. Lan gained back a little of the weight she had lost and had begun going back to classes. But she did not stay well for long.

Two weeks after returning to the dormitory, Lan developed a high fever and shaking chills. This time she was diagnosed as having malaria. Again, she was the only one in the entire dormitory to contract the illness, and there were no mosquitoes to speak of. At this point, my parents decided that Lan probably would not survive the winter. And they worried they could no longer afford to pay our tuition. After Lan got over the malaria, we packed up and headed for home. It was a great relief to return to the comfort and shelter of our home. I realized that it was not fun at all to be on my own and I began to appreciate even more the heavy burden my parents carried on their shoulders.

A few days after we got home, Lan began to itch all over, and her skin broke out in red patches. Dr. Zhang the only Western-trained doctor in town, was summoned. My father had a tremendous admiration for the doctor. He had always taken care of our family, treating us for everything from hookworm to trachoma to childbirth. He was known to have performed leg amputation and appendectomy without anesthesia. What Lan had, we were told, was scabies.

Again I was baffled as to how Lan had gotten the disease, but it must have come from someone in school. True to the old Chinese saying: "Better to sleep in the same bed with a leper than to live next door to scabies." The scabies, caused by tiny spider-like creatures that burrowed under the skin, quickly spread to the entire household.

The cure for scabies, according to Dr. Zhang, was simple. First, we undressed in front of a stove. Then we sprinkled yellow sulfur powder on a piece of lard, wrapped it in a piece of gauze and heated it over the stove. When the oil and sulfur began to ooze out, we quickly rubbed it all over our bodies. Our clothes had to be boiled before laundering.

Actually we had a lot of fun with this remedy, giggling in front of the fire like primitives. We all smelled like rotten eggs, but we were cured.

Lan and I never returned to Yantai to finish our last two years of high school. It was near the end of the war, there were severe food shortages and inflation was rampant. On pay days, Yisheng, my eldest younger brother, had to wait by the door of Father's office. As soon as Father handed over the money, Yisheng would run as fast as he could to the grain store to buy sacks of corn flour. By the afternoon, the price would have risen several times.

The news coming from the front was distressing. The Japanese had stepped up their military assault, and fighting with the Americans in the Pacific was fierce. Our home town, Changsha, which had until then bravely resisted the Japanese aggression, finally fell. Numerous soldiers and civilians were killed during three consecutive seesaw fighting and hand-to-hand combats on the street. The enemy was pointing towards

Chongqing, the Nationalist war-time capital. The Japanese soldiers on the streets of Weihai were getting younger. The older ones were all on the front lines. The soldiers were not as proud and confident as before, and their uniforms were shabby. It looked like something was going to happen. My parents wanted us to be home in anticipation of more turbulent times ahead.

One day, Mother took Nai Nai and Lin Ma to see a fortuneteller. Their nerves were frazzled by the war, and they wanted to know their fate. Each had left an only son at home. They were fearful that their sons would either be killed by the Japanese or starve to death. For them, that would be the worst of all possible fates, to have no one to sweep the family grave, to worship the ancestors on holidays, and to carry on the family name.

The blind fortuneteller and his family lived in a modest traditional house with a central court surrounded on three sides by small rooms. In the anteroom, there was a table displaying a small golden statue of a god, candles and incense. The women were led to the adjoining small room, where a middle-aged blind man in blue cotton peasant clothing sat cross-legged on top of a brick bed. He looked like an ordinary working-class man.

The women were seated in chairs across from the fortuneteller. They started by telling the blind man their eight letters (year, month, date and hour of their birth), but despite Lin Ma's loud, resonant voice, the man could not understand her Hunan dialect. My mother, who spoke Mandarin, had to act as a translator. At the time, the only people in town who did not speak the local dialect were either working for the government or in the military.

The man took out a bundle of bamboo sticks with symbols engraved on them and asked each of the two old ladies to draw three sticks. With a concentrated look on his face, he read the bamboo sticks with his finger tips and matched the symbols with the eight letters. After he had finished his calculations, he slowly began his pronouncements.

He started with Lin Ma. "Your eight letters are good and strong; your fate is very good," the fortuneteller said. The women, caught by surprise, fell silent.

"You were born into a wealthy family. All your life you have had money and honor, no bitterness," said the fortuneteller. Again silence.

"You have married a military man, a General," he continued. More silence.

"What about my son?" asked Lin Ma.

But the fortuneteller did not understand her, and again, Mother translated for him. The Chinese language does not distinguish singular from plural nouns, so the question could have been taken to mean, "what about my sons?"

"In your fate you have six children and twenty six grandchildren," he replied.

"When can I go back to my old home?" Lin Ma wanted to know.

"Your life will be unsettled until you are sixty-three, then you will return to your old home and enjoy a peaceful life with your sons and grandsons."

Later that day, as our mother retold the story, she had an amused look on her face, her curiosity satisfied. Just as she had suspected, this fortuneteller was another one of the so-called "wanderers along the rivers and lakes." They were street-wise people who could size up a person by their looks or their manner of speech. The man was out of his element this time because he could neither see nor understand our dialect and therefore could not distinguish Lin Ma's peasant talk from Nai Nai's soft spoken, refined language. Nai Nai looked downcast and said nothing all evening. I suspected that her fate, according to the fortuneteller, may not have been as glamorous as Lin Ma's.

For once in her life, Lin Ma was the talk of the day. She was both puzzled and pleased about the fortuneteller's version of her fate. Perhaps she wanted to believe that God had intended for her to marry a rich and powerful husband and to have many children and grandchildren. But something had gone wrong and she was at a loss to explain what it was. She had one unshakeable belief though: "I am going home, I want to eat the Hunan rice and the wild mushrooms before I die."

ADDENDUM:

The first Sino-Japanese war took place on Master Liu's island located at the mouth of Weihai bay. The island was both the naval base and home to the newly established North Sea Naval Academy. The picturesque island is four miles long and one and half miles wide. Its east side faces the choppy Yellow sea and the west shore is only two nautical miles away from Weihai.

In 1894, a military confrontation developed between Chinese and Japanese armies in Korea over a domestic conflict. Both countries had claimed to be Korea's protector. The Chinese army was defeated. Then the Japanese navy sailed sixty miles across the strait to attack the China North Sea fleet that had retreated from Korea to Master Liu's island.

As the Japanese Navy assault the island, Japanese troops totaling 200,000 men made a surprise landing on the Shandong peninsula and marched towards Weihai. Under heavy fire from land and sea, the entire Chinese Navy consisting of two battleships, ten cruisers and two torpedo boats, was decimated. Most of the thirty new graduates of the Naval Academy were lost at sea. The Chinese Naval Commander Ding Yuzhong and two senior Admirals committed suicide. The Qing government sued for peace.

The peace treaty, mediated by the preeminent statesman and founder of the modern Chinese Navy, Li Hongzhang, was to be a disaster for China and a huge military and economic victory for Japan. Besides paying two hundred million silver dollars as war compensation and the granting of many special privileges including railroad rights and "the most favorite nation status," China was to cede to Japan, in perpetuity, the island of Taiwan.

Chapter 6

THE STRUGGLE

The war with Japan dragged on for eight years with no end in sight. It looked as if God had willed 450 million Chinese to die either by violence or starvation.

One day in late summer of 1945, Father came home from work earlier than usual. As he hurried through the courtyard, he yelled: "Children, the war is over! Japan has surrendered!" It sounded like a decree from heaven: "Children, you shall live!" At the time, the end of the war was, to me, as incomprehensible as its beginning. We could hardly contain our joy and excitement, but people dared not to celebrate while the Japanese were still in town.

For a few days, Father's face lit up with rare smiles. Rumors came through the grapevine that in Beijing and Shanghai, the Japanese had peacefully surrendered to the Nationalist Army. We were anxiously waiting for the same thing to happen. But then we heard the sporadic rumbling of cannons, like distant thunder, coming from beyond the hills. People stayed behind closed doors for fear of an imminent battle on the streets. After several days, the fireworks abruptly stopped. The streets were eerily quiet. Soon we heard feet shuffling outside our doors. It was the sound of the Japanese army in retreat.

Almost as soon as the last Japanese soldier had left town, in marched the victors. They turned out to be soldiers of the Communist 8th Route Army, dressed in shabby, grey uniforms with red stars on their caps. The townspeople lined the streets, lighting firecrackers and playing drums and gongs to celebrate victory over the Japanese, and to give a hero's welcome to our Chinese soldiers. But even amidst the victory, there was an air of uncertainty. No one knew what was coming next, and they were bracing for more turmoil ahead.

The Communists wasted no time in arresting the officials who had served in the Japanese puppet regime. Then rumors began to circulate that the Communists were going to launch a campaign against what they called "class enemies:" the rich, the landowners, the bourgeoisie—anyone whom they regarded as oppressors of the poor. People on the street looked nervous, and tension was felt everywhere. The Customs House was closed, since there was no business, but the employee did not remain idle. They had to go to the office every day to get indoctrinated about the Communist cause. My father, who had a lot of exposure to Communism in his youth, had to play humble in front of the young *ganbu*, or Communist cadres. Most were barely literate peasants who had never set foot outside of the farm. In private, the *ganbu* were referred to as *tubaozhi* (mud pie). Father had to write lengthy self-criticisms, in which he admitted his past errors of serving the bourgeoisie and collaborating with the imperialist enemies. While all this political indoctrination was going on, none of the employees of the Custom's House was drawing a salary. My father lost the income that had sustained our family of fifteen.

But people did not despair. They always kept an eye on the horizon where the choppy sounds of airplanes were occasionally heard. Someone claimed to have spotted bombers with American emblems circling over Master Liu's island. One day the unexpected happened: an American fighter plane on a reconnaissance mission crashed into the sea. According to eyewitnesses, two American pilots had parachuted and landed on the water. When the officials arrived at the scene in a motorboat, the pilots were struggling in the choppy waves. The officials cut off the engine and watched until the pilots went under.

A few days later, the town was suddenly seized with excitement. People turned out in droves on the beach to watch an American warship, the size of which no one had ever seen, slowly sailing into the harbor. Its dark grey hull, almost blocking the inlet of the bay, was shrouded in an aura of impenetrable power and mystery.

Several Chinese officials came to our house to fetch our father. Father hurriedly changed into his Western suit and went out with the officials. They boarded a speedboat and went to the American ship where Father acted as a translator. After several days of talks, the Americans were satisfied with the explanation about the lost airplane. As the warship disappeared over the horizon, so went our hopes.

Father was close-mouthed about what had transpired on the American ship. The only thing I heard him say was that the American Naval officers had addressed him as the "Professor."

The Communist officials had recognized Father's linguistic and diplomatic skills. They asked him to go to Yan'an, the seat of the Communists' power, to work as a diplomat. Realizing his responsibility to his family, Father turned down the offer. I didn't know at the time that Father had ties with some top people in Yan'an. Decades later, I learned that the preeminent Communist diplomat Lin Zuhan (or Lin Baijue), who had mediated peace negotiations with the Nationalists and US Ambassador Patrick Hurley, was a close family friend.

The Communist government did not let people starve. We were given a ration of twenty-five pounds of grain per person each month. But it was barely edible, just moldy corn or *gauliang* (red sorghum) mixed with gravel. We had to sift the grain in a pan to separate the gravel, then we tossed it in the air and blew off the dust and mold. We paid our neighbor to use his stone mill to grind the grain into flour. We five older girls took turns walking around the mill and pushing a wooden stick to turn the four-feet-wide stone slabs. It was hard work and made us seasick.

We longed for the easy, comfortable life before the war, and wondered if we would ever see days like that again. Lin Ma, in her usual moralistic tone, told us that the reason we were having a hard time was because our family had already used up our store of *fu*, or luck. To Lin Ma, *fu* comes in a predestined package which is exhaustible. A person has to save his *fu*, use it sparingly and add to it by worshiping god and doing charitable deeds.

To raise cash to buy vegetables and fuel, we opened a business in the flea market. Items of no immediate use such as fur coats, silk robes, vases, books, cameras, memorabilia and trinkets were all taken out for sale. These luxury items, rarely seen in the backwoods of Shandong, attracted many buyers. We actually had a lot of fun playing shopkeeper and bringing home the money.

The officials wasted no time in establishing a political system to indoctrinate the public about the ideals of Communism. They organized families into neighborhood groups, and each group had a representative. Every few days, the representative, usually a housewife, would come to the door and relay messages from the Communist leadership.

One crisp autumn day, I represented my family and attended my first "struggle meeting." I went to the Big Field carrying a little stool, and sat down amongst rows of local men and women. On their honest and plain faces were signs of bewilderment and anxiety. A group of cadres, dressed in Mao uniforms, had set a five-foot-high platform in front of the seated audience. A young cadre went to the front of the platform and gave an animated speech about how the old, evil society had allowed wicked people to enslave others. He declared the following as enemies of the people: landlords, owners of shops and brothels and people working for foreigners. On hearing this last category, I lowered my head and my stomach tightened into a knot.

The first person to be struggled against was a landowner. A middle-aged, plump man was led to the platform with hands tied behind his back. He was told to get on the platform and kneel down. His accuser, an emaciated tenant farmer, began telling the story of how the landowner had taken all the grain his family had harvested, leaving practically nothing for them to live on. When the landowner started to say something in his own defense, the official stopped the proceeding, and ordered a table be placed on top of the platform. A second table was added, and then a third, and the man was ordered to climb the structure, balancing precariously as he reached the top. The leader asked the accused to admit to his crime. When no answer came, the leader suddenly pulled a rope that was tied to one leg of the bottom table, causing the tables to collapse and the man to crash to the ground.

As the man cried out in pain, I had the same sickening feeling as I did while watching Lin Ma slaughter a chicken. I had to lower my eyes and hide my tears. The audience was deadly silent; no one uttered a sound. Anyone who showed sympathy would be found as guilty as the accused man.

The cadres dragged in their next target, a middle-aged woman with messy hair and rumpled clothing. She was the former owner of a brothel on the 13th Avenue, the red light district. A young woman in the audience got up and tearfully described how the brothel owner had forced the girls to entertain an unbroken stream of men day and night. If they did not perform satisfactorily, they would be beaten and their skin scorched with burning incense. As the brothel owner was brought crashing to the ground, the young woman covered her face with her hands and started sobbing. As a finale, they brought a bucket of night soil and pushed the landowner's head into it. The man emerged gagging and gasping for breath.

Despite the bright autumn sun, I felt cold chills running down my spine. My sympathy for the poor farmer and the unfortunate girl could not persuade me to swallow the Communists' way of using violence to achieve justice. I had always been aware of a strong streak of violence in my people, a trait that Confucians tried to curb through teachings of humanity, civility and self-restraint. To denounce the old teachings and to unleash the pent-up violence lurking in the Chinese soul was to court disaster.

From what I knew about Chinese history, even tyrannical governments and foreign conquerors would leave people alone as long as they did not commit a crime or engage in subversive activities. But according to the Communists, it was a crime to be born into the wrong kind of family. They graded people on the basis of their *zu sheng* or social class: poor farmers were on top, while landowners, wealthy merchants and intellectuals were at the bottom. People of "bad birth" were branded for life; they were prohibited from getting a good education, or a good job, so consequently no one wanted to marry them. There was no way they could get ahead.

At the age of fifteen, I made up my mind that I did not want to live in a world like that.

The long cold winter was filled with despair. Our food supply was dwindling. We were surviving on a shoestring and had no idea how long it was going to last.

One bitter cold winter morning, an unusual commotion descended upon our household. Nai Nai chased the children out of Mother's room and told my brother to go fetch Dr. Zhang. Lin Ma was boiling water in the kitchen. I was terrified that Mother was sick again. But then elder sister Yu said: "Mother is going to give birth!"

"A baby? At her age?" I was embarrassed and couldn't believe that a thirty-eight-year-old woman could make babies. Her figure did not show under her loose gown and she hadn't gained any weight. I was worried sick as I remembered a horrendous tale Lin Ma had told me. It was about a woman who howled for days and could not bring the baby into the world. When the woman finally died, they had to carry her out the door, feet first, with a wooden board covering her swollen belly to keep the bloody *qi* contained inside her.

After waiting for hours in the living room across the hall, I heard low moans and panting that lasted about twenty minutes. Then there was silence and my heart sank. Minutes later, I heard a baby's weak cry. Thank god, they made it. Miraculously, the baby girl was well developed although she was slender and delicate. Even though times were hard, the birth of a baby was always a blessing in a Chinese household. The baby was named Yuan, meaning "circle" or "complete." The implication was that the family was complete.

But there was more to come.

A month later First Aunt gave birth to a baby girl, the tenth child in our family, a round figure. The baby's name was Mang, meaning "full."

For the two nursing mothers, Lin Ma killed our last hen and made chicken soup. While Mother was confined to bed, I took charge of my baby sister, hand washed the diapers and put them near the stove to dry. Although the babies provided much joy and distraction, the atmosphere was grim.

One day, my father had a serious talk with Lan and I. What weighed most heavily on his mind, besides our daily essentials, was the fact that we were high school dropouts. Under normal circumstances, we would be in our last year of high school preparing for college. Before the war, Father had put away, in the Chinese Central Bank, several hundred silver dollars, more than enough for college. He still had the bank receipt, but by then it was worthless. He doubted that he would ever get his life's savings back.

"I never dreamed that I would not be able to send you to college!" His voice was cracking.

After that, Lan and I had a private talk between us. We

decided that we would not allow circumstance to dictate our future. Someday, we declared, we will go on to college. But first, we had to keep up with our studies. We set up a schedule like the school calendar. We read, from cover to cover, all the high school textbooks: Chinese, English, history, geography, chemistry, physics, trigonometry, biology and algebra. We made sure we understood what we read, could answer the questions and solve the mathematical problems.

That year, the electric power plant was closed down, and we were without electricity. We read during the day and in the evening, continued our studies by the light of a cotton cord soaked in a dish of cooking oil. In one year, we had made up for the two missing years of high school.

By the spring of 1946, we had come to the end of our rope. The food supplies and coal in the storage room were all gone. Except for Mother's jewelry, anything of value had already been sold. Our family of fifteen was facing the grim prospect of starvation. One evening I went into the study to get a book, and was surprised to find my father sitting alone in the dark. In the fading light, his face was shiny with tears. Not wanting to embarrass him, I left quickly. I was shocked and frightened to see my resourceful father reduced to tears!

Father's colleagues were running into the same difficulties although no one had nearly as large a family as ours. The men pondered about the hopelessness of the situation and decided to make a break. With considerable trepidation, my father and a colleague, the top two men in the company, went to the Communist cadre and asked for permission to move their families back to their hometowns in the south. Surprisingly, not only did they allow us to leave, but the government even paid for the moving expenses. For weeks, everyone was excited and running in high gear. My mother collected a bag of rags for sister Yu to paste them into boards. She cut out the boards into multiple layers and stitched them together with twine to make cloth shoes to wear on the road. The shoes looked like ordinary shoes but there was a catch.

They had holes cut in the center of the soles for Mother to hide gold bracelets, jade rings and pearl earrings.

We had to part with everything that had no survival value. We left with only our quilts, rice bowls, chopsticks, two woks, a few kitchen utensils, and a few trunks of clothes. I remember taking a last long look at our house and feeling the pain of leaving all the things that were dear to me. It was a defining moment in my life. From that point on, I willed myself not to become overly attached to earthly possessions, knowing that sooner or later I might have to give them up. I would carry my valuables and my secrets inside myself, so no one could take them away.

At the time, I had no clear idea where we were going, and how would we get there. To get to Hunan we would have to go to Qingdao, then on to Shanghai and Changsha; all three cities were controlled by Nationalists. The land in between was a patchwork of territories occupied by Communists, and in some places the fighting still raged. Even if we could reach Hunan unscathed, would we have a better chance of survival? Could we claim the land and the old house our family used to own? Could our father find a job? Would we be able to go to college? I didn't know and I didn't think my parents knew the answers either. In their desperation, they had decided to take a chance and leave the rest to fate.

We left on a grey spring morning, the Liu family of fifteen, ranging in age from six months to sixty. We traveled with my father's colleague, Mr. Hu and his family of four. At a time when motor vehicles were hard to come by, we were grateful to have two ancient, dilapidated open trucks, one for passengers and the other for luggage. The adults were seated on fixed wooden benches along the sides while the children sat on the floor on top of rolls of bedding. Father counted the heads to make sure no one was left behind.

As the trucks pulled away, I saw Blackie running toward us. She was wide-eyed and panting; her ears were flat against the sides of her head. I looked at Father and waited for him to order the driver to stop and let Blackie in. But Father looked away, his eyes brimming with tears.

Blackie had come to us soon after we had moved to Weihai. The cute black puppy followed Father home one day and decided that she belonged to us. She was considered a good omen as dogs always follow *fu*. Father must have felt that he and the dog had *yuan*, a connection during a previous life.

Blackie had short, shiny black fur, soft brown eyes and a disposition too sweet to be a watchdog. Luckily, there were no street crimes even though people were starving. Blackie never barked at anyone except the beggars who came to the door several times a day. One was a middle-aged, toothless man, dressed in rags who walked with a limp and a long "dog-beating" stick in hand. He made a daily routine of coming to the door and bellowing out in a resonant baritone voice: "Three day no food, Madam, Aye.... yah...." He would go on and on until Lin Ma dished out some leftovers from the kitchen. Blackie eventually got used to the man and stopped the symbolic barking. Later, my brothers found out that the three-day-no-food man was not starving at all. He threw the food scraps to his pigs, which he raised and sold for a profit.

Blackie made a routine of waiting for Father outside his office and walking home with him twice a day. She knew who was the boss, but kept a respectable distance from the kids. She was very content to have two square meals a day and a mat to sleep on in the hallway inside the gate. Lin Ma fed her scraps from the table which in the good old days were tasty and nutritious. Even during the hard times, Blackie did not go hungry, for she was one of the children. Lin Ma would sooner take food out of her own mouth than let the dog starve.

I was to be haunted for the rest of my life by the image of Blackie chasing after us in that open truck. It felt as if we had abandoned a child!

From Weihai, our trucks headed south on country roads. It was mild late spring weather with a warm gentle breeze.

GRANDFATHER'S MICROSCOPE

The trucks chugged along slowly, emitting dense fumes from their coal-burning fuel tanks. Each time our trucks struggled to go up a hill, we all had to get off and walk.

I was holding my baby sister, swathed in a little quilt. Nai Nai was cursing as usual, about the truck, the road and the weather. She had hated Shandong since she first set foot on it ten years earlier. To her, Shandong was *chong shan e' shui*, meaning barren mountains and menacing rivers. Shandong could not begin to compare with the lush green hills and gentle lakes of her hometown. Somehow Nai Nai and Lin Ma both held on to the belief that once they reached their native soil, their misery would be over.

We were heading towards Laiyang, an inland farming town that had been a Communist stronghold during the war. The region was famous for its sweet and juicy pears.

My father negotiated with the local Communist authorities about our trip back home to Hunan. From Laiyang, we had to cross the front lines into the Nationalist-controlled coastal city of Qingdao only eighty miles to the east. But there were no trucks or cars traveling on that stretch of no-man's land.

So we abandoned our open trucks and began our journey towards Qingdao with a caravan of twelve wheelbarrows, nine for passengers and the rest for luggage. Father was in front with my second younger brother Yijian. Lan rode opposite Nai Nai. Lin Ma rode with her favorite, my eldest younger brother Yisheng. I carried the baby opposite Mother. As a physically fit young woman, I was embarrassed to have someone push me, but I had to balance the wheelbarrow.

The drivers were short, sturdy young men with bundles of muscles protruding from their arms and legs. They wore straw sandals that gave a good traction on the dirt road, and they easily pushed the wheelbarrows with short running steps. The weather was sunny and cool, perfect for traveling. We wound our way through a landscape of level farms, which seemed deserted. There were few travelers on the road. The awkward silence was broken only when one of the drivers hummed a nameless folk song. The procession took breaks at roadside stands for lunch and boiled water. In the afternoon, the drivers slowed down and showed signs of fatigue, their leg muscles bulged under the strain of their loads. The wheelbarrows got separated, and some drivers ran ahead of others. Eventually we all congregated at a rustic inn. We had an early supper and the whole family slept in one huge brick bed.

The second day started out gloomy and clouds were gathering overhead. By mid-afternoon, the sky became dark and menacing. As the rain began to pour down, the dirt road turned into a slippery, sticky yellow paste. Our driver was slipping and sliding in the mud. All the passengers had to get off and walk. I carried the baby in my left arm and steadied my mother with my right arm while keeping my eyes on the ground in front of me. When I finally looked up, all I could see was a narrow muddy road surrounded by tall red sorghum. The other wheelbarrows were nowhere in sight.

Silently, we struggled on through the slippery mud and the downpour until it became dark. There was no light anywhere. I had no idea where we were or how long it would take to reach an inn. A sense of doom had crept up on me. I feared my mother and baby sister might not make it. I was also worried about Nai Nai and Lin Ma who had not stepped outside of the front gate in years. How could they manage through the mud with their tiny feet?

Finally I heard voices in the distance. As we got closer, I was relieved to see the slender figure of Nai Nai waddling in the mud. She was hanging on to Lan with one hand and holding a handkerchief over her head with the other. Periodically, she would point a finger toward the sky, shrieking and cursing:

"You! You give me a hard time again! *Chien dao wan sha*!" That bloodcurdling curse meant: "You deserve to be sliced by thousand knives and die ten thousand deaths!" The "you" meant "heaven."

I was used to hearing Nai Nai cursing, but this was the first time I had heard her curse heaven. I worried that she was taking her complaints too far.

It was not too long before I saw a faint light coming from a farmhouse ahead. As we got closer, a whiff of cooked chives, indescribably inviting, drifted into my nostrils. When we arrived at this lonely inn, the rest of the family, all soaking wet and exhausted, was gathering in front of a huge wood-burning stove. The whole inn was one large room with a stove in the center and two large brick beds, one on either end of the room. At first, we were glad there were no other travelers in the inn that night. Then the innkeeper told us why it was so quiet. The night before, armed robbers had come and killed several people. Too exhausted to care, we were resigned to fate.

We took off our wet outer clothes and shoes and hung them around the stove to dry. Then we had the most delicious meal in memory: a large plate of steamed buns, with crispy fried bottoms, made of white flour and stuffed with chives and cubes of fat pork. That night the two families slept in one brick bed while the drivers slept in the other. We were packed like sardines with hardly any room to turn around. But it was warm and dry and I slept soundly.

Everyone woke up at dawn and after breakfast we were on the road again. Ten minutes into the journey, Lan suddenly leapt off her seat and ran back toward the inn. She had left her wet shoes next to the stove. We all waited silently knowing that Mother's jewelry was hidden in those shoes. Fortunately, no one had taken the muddy shoes and we were again on our way. We were lucky that Lan remembered the shoes in time; the jewelry turned out to be life sustaining in later years.

Tension mounted as we approached the border between Nationalist- and Communist-occupied territories. After traveling for miles on deserted roads, we were suddenly confronted by uniformed guards who had no red stars on their caps. They were better dressed than the Red Army soldiers.

My heart was in my throat as Father came forward to show our papers. I was thinking, "what if they won't let us in?" The guards looked at the papers briefly and waved us on. I could see relief spreading over my father's face. The wheelbarrow pushers unloaded our luggage and went back where they came from. A truck appeared out of nowhere and took us to the city of Qingdao.

My first impression of this metropolitan city was disbelief and awe. The Western-styled concrete buildings, several stories tall, and fast automobiles on the wide tar-topped roads, stunned me. For the very first time, I saw jaunty American sailors walking on the streets or sitting in rickshaws pulled by coolies half their size.

I didn't know at the time that Qingdao was always our final destination. Father never intended to go back to Hunan where there was no prospect of finding a job. It was just a ruse to persuade the Communists to let us leave. As long as the Nationalists let us through the city gate, this was where we were to stay.

Father went straight to the Custom's House and reported for duty. We were then taken to a high-rise apartment building that housed thirty employees and their families. Our apartment was on the top (fourth) floor. From the staircase landing, we had a nice view of this beautiful city with its hilly streets and red-roofed Western-style houses.

Our apartment was Japanese-style, compact and efficient, with three small rooms, a tiny kitchen and a bath. We could sit, eat and sleep on the Tatami floor and did not need to buy furniture. It was the very first time we saw "automatic water" coming out of a faucet, a flush toilet and a propane stove Lin Ma could light with a match. Father started working the next day and was given an advance stipend. It was like the good old days again. We could afford to buy white rice, white flour, meat and vegetables. With great relief, our family settled down and made no plans to go anywhere.

Having solved the immediate problems of food and shelter, we started to look for schools. We were told about a public high school just a block away from our apartment. The school, named Guo Hua (Nation's Light), was newly established by the Nationalist government to accommodate refugee students from the Communist-occupied territories. The tuition was free, and we only needed our school records to get in.

In May of 1946, the seven of us, four girls and three boys, went to register. I was delighted to see old friends from Weihai and Yantai who had also come to Qingdao with their families. Our former classmates were seniors in high school now, and they would soon graduate and be eligible for college. Lan and I had missed nearly two years of high school, and should have been placed in the junior class. But we told the registrar that we were in the same senior class as the other girls, but we had lost our school records during our escape. The school let us in.

The school was previously the site of a Japanese Shinto temple. It had stone-paved, winding paths that led to scattered pagodas and monuments up the hill. Classes were conducted in an open field, and on rainy days, in the former meditation hall or in the pagodas. The senior class had only a dozen students. During the month of June that year, Lan and I spent every minute of our waking hours pouring over the books. We had no problem passing the high school graduation examination nor the highly competitive entrance examination to National Shandong University, the only university in town.

I could not pinpoint the exact time, but it must have been around eighth grade when my parents put the idea into my head that I should be a doctor. In the beginning, it was just a hint, and over time it developed into an open discussion. They said that I had the characteristics needed to become a doctor: I was strong, kind-hearted and a good student in science. But each time I went to a doctor's office, the austere atmosphere, the shiny steel instruments and the smell of Lysol made me afraid. I didn't want to be a doctor until Lan had her close brush with death in high school. Without hesitation, I went and registered as a freshman in the medical school.

My parents were uncertain about the direction of Lan's future. Although a good student in science, her heart and talent were in the arts. But Shandong University did not have an art department, and the famous art institutes in Shanghai and in Hangzhou were beyond our means. Besides, my parents had misgivings about the practicality of the humanities in a world full of turbulence. Even in good times, an artist was likely to be unemployed and live in poverty. It was a particularly unsuitable profession for a first-born child who has the obligation to help the parents raise the younger siblings. Finally it was decided that Lan should play it safe and choose a career that guaranteed her employment. When Lan went to register in the engineering department, she was surprised to find she was the only female student. The professor told Lan that she might feel very uncomfortable in an all male group and advised her to change her major. Without much conviction, Lan switched to chemistry where there were at least a handful of female students.

We heard there was money to be made painting portraits for American sailors. Lan got hold of an agent who would bring photographs of American sailors for her to paint. She bought canvas and tubes of oil paint, and set up shop in our tiny living room. Although it was the first time she had done oil portraits, her paintings were true to life and quite presentable. For each portrait which took an average of two days to complete, Lan was paid ten US dollars, half of which went to the middleman. Lan gave all the money to Mother who in turn gave Lan and me an allowance. With money in our pockets, we went downtown shopping for new clothes and shoes for school.

Ever since that pitch-dark night when Nai Nai stood in the driving rain, pointing a crooked finger toward the sky and cursing heaven, I had been worried about a reprimand from the Gods. But Nai Nai had won, our lives had taken a 180-degree turn. Father was able to arrange for friends to take Nai Nai and Lin Ma back to their hometown, and their decade-long wish was finally granted. Meanwhile, Lan and I danced in our new leather shoes to the university to begin our freshman year, the dreamiest year of our lives.

Family picture taken in Qindao just before Lin Ma went back to the old home. Back row, left to right: Yijien, Father, Yisheng, Mei, Na, Lien. Second row, left to right: Lin Ma, Lan, Yu, Mother, Yiwu. Front row, left to right: Fong (half sister) and Yuan. Mei was eighteen years old, a first year medical student. Circa 1947. Photograph by Father.

Chapter 7

UNDER THE PEACH BLOSSOMS

As soon as I set foot on the campus of Shandong University, I was walking on air. After so many years of struggling in a chaotic world, I had finally made it to college. I was ready and eager to pursue my college education.

The university was located on "Fish Hill Road," within walking distance of the beach and a beautiful Seaside Park. Before the city fell to the Japanese, the entire university—faculty, staff and students—had picked up and moved with the Nationalist government to the rear of the fighting in the mountainous west. At the end of the war, with the economy in shambles, the returning school officials were faced with the seemingly insurmountable task of rebuilding the institution almost from the ground up. Within two years, however, they had accomplished nothing short of a miracle. The school recruited a host of renowned scholars to fill faculty positions. To supplement limited government funding, the school raised cash by renting part of its real estate to the U.S. Marines. The $10,000 US dollar monthly rent paid for the books and laboratory equipment purchased from the U.S. The chancellor and dean of our university, appointees of the Nationalist government, were nationally renowned liberal-minded scholars. Nowhere could one find a group of students more enthusiastic and appreciative than we were.

Qingdao was once a German colony. When Britain annexed Hong Kong, Germany, on the grounds that two German missionaries had been killed in the province, occupied Qingdao and forced the Qing government to sign an agreement leasing the city, along with railroad and mining rights in the province, for 99 years. Christian and Catholic missionaries built schools, hospitals, and foreign investors built factories, including the famous Qingdao beer brewery. The city was known for its efficient administration, graceful seashore, and its beautiful, European-style buildings.

Now, the "imperialist enemies" and the humiliating unequal treaties were gone; Japan had been defeated as well. It was a heady time for us. We were all eager to get on with our studies so that we could help rebuild the country. We wanted to be the first generation of Chinese who were truly masters of our own destinies. To live in a strong and free China was every Chinese person's dream.

For the first time, my parents were genuinely happy. They shared with Lan and me our excitement about going to college, and were eager to participate in our hopes and dreams. In the evenings, when I sat at the dining table doing my homework, Father would now and then peek over my shoulder or leaf through my medical books, with pride, satisfaction, and envy on his face. I had to tell him about things that went on in school, the courses and the professors. Life was so joyous and full that I had no wish for any distractions, least of all romance. But fate had decided that I was to run into what we called "peach blossom fate," predestined romance.

I had missed my very first biology lab session on account of a basketball game. I was the captain of the university women's basketball team, and played center forward. I had tried to get out of the game, but the Coach would not hear of it. Without me, he said, we would surely lose the game and the championship. The Coach, an influential man, said he would talk with our biology teacher and ask him to let me make it up later. Reluctantly, I went along and we won the city-wide championship.

When I showed up at the door of the biology department the following day, I was very nervous. For the first time in my seventeen years of life, I was about to face a grown-up man unescorted. Besides, I had been warned that the assistant professor, Mr. Yen, was tough and bad-tempered. It worried me that he might resent being put upon.

When Mr. Yen came forward to meet me, his physical appearance took me by surprise. A slightly built man in his mid-twenties, he was dressed in a Western-style tweed jacket. His large, bright eyes exuded intelligence and passion. He spoke a suave Shanghai-accented Mandarin, and his genuine smile at once put me at ease.

After seating me at a table, Mr. Yen unlocked a cabinet, brought out a microscope and placed it in front of me. Then he brought out a tray, and on it were glass slides, cover-slips, forceps, dissecting needles and a yellow onion. He removed the dry skin from the onion, took out a white layer and striped off the outer membrane. Using the forceps, he spread out the thin membrane between two glass slides, and placed it under the microscope. When I peered through the eyepiece, I was struck by a spectacular sight: a compact sheet of identical cells, polygonal in shape and translucent under the reflected light from the window. Next, he handed me a tongue depressor, and told me to gently rub it against the inside of my cheek, and smear it on a slide. As I hesitated, he discreetly walked away.

What I saw in my saliva under the microscope was even more astonishing; it looked almost the same as the onion skin. I couldn't believe that human cells and vegetable cells were constructed the same way: tiny cell units, each with a cytoplasm and a nucleus that contained genetic material. I made sketches and wrote descriptions of what I saw and handed in my lab report.

When I walked out of the room, I felt giddy and my face was flushed. I was galvanized by a vague feeling that this day would be one of the most memorable ones in my life. I couldn't wait to get home and share with my father the thrill of seeing the "invisible things" under the microscope. I felt as if a mystery from my childhood had been solved.

I remembered one lazy Sunday afternoon when I was ten, we all had nothing to do. My father went to the storage room and took out a large wooden box. He unlocked the box with a key and carefully took out a curious object made of a shiny copper tube mounted on a black metal stand. Father placed it in the center of the dining table as if it were a sacred object. Then he summoned all the children. While we stood around the table examining this curiosity, Father declared in a lecturing tone: "This is a microscope. Your grandfather brought it back from overseas. It enables you to see things that are invisible to your eyes."

My grandfather was not a doctor, nor a scientist. I was aware he was some kind of lawyer. Beyond that I knew little about the man, because he died before I was born.

Father did not know how to work the microscope. I was left wondering what those "invisible things" were. Ghosts, maybe? Fathers added: "Some day, this will belong to whomever takes up a career in medicine." By then I was even more puzzled about the connection between ghosts and medicine. Nonetheless, the image of the microscope, mysterious and golden, was forever engraved in my memory.

Mr. Yen turned out to be a very likable person. Unlike his peers, who were severe and reserved, he was sociable, energetic, and full of laughter. He loved to talk to students after classes. To me in particular, he showered attention. During lab sessions, he made frequent stops by my desk to check my progress. He often showed up at the athletic field where I was practicing basketball and volleyball, and chatted with my sister and me.

The attention I got from the instructor did not pass unnoticed. Other young men in my class made only tentative moves to get my attention, but I was totally uninterested. However, my relationship with Yen remained proper and restrained. We never had a private moment together. I knew nothing about him except that he had gone to college in the rear of the fighting during the war. He was a man of the world, a restless intellectual with a passionate interest in everything. In his presence, I felt like a child: shy, naive and inexperienced. I thought the world of him, but I was torn by conflicted feelings. I wanted to be guided and protected, but I was also afraid of being dominated and of losing control over my own destiny. What's more, I sensed that he was a dangerous man. He spoke with euphoria about anti-government movements on campus, and as time went by, I began to suspect that he might have been one of the leaders in the leftist movement that was about to erupt nationwide.

Toward the end of my freshman year, the first of many anti-government demonstrations broke out on campus. For days, classes were suspended and I had to stay home. The day when the classes resumed, I came across Mr. Yen in front of our classroom talking enigmatically with a group of students. He was standing under a blossoming peach tree, his face flushed and eyes sparkling. He was recounting with relish the details of the student demonstration and of the confrontation with the police. I stood there watching him and my heart was filled with a sense of doom.

"If only those students knew what it is like to live under Communism!" These words left my mouth even before I had time to think.

Mr. Yen was startled by my remark. His smile froze, then faded away. No one asked me to explain myself. In that instant, I saw an invisible wall appearing between us. Neither of us said anything further.

In the years to come, the scene under the peach blossoms would resurface in my mind innumerable times. I came to realize that on that day, a fork in the road appeared before me, and I took a decisive step down one path. It's a decision that sealed my fate. To this day, I still don't know if I was led to this decision by a dream.

I was hiding behind a bush watching a crowd of people milling about in an open field. I knew I was in danger and had to keep quiet. A column of soldiers marched into view and the two men in front carried a wooden chest which they placed on the ground. They opened the chest and took riffles out of it. Then three vicious dogs jumped out of the chest and headed straight for me. I started running along a narrow path surrounded by black volcanic rock until I came to a seashore. I saw a man standing on a rock jutting out into the water. It was Yen. He turned to look at me, his face filled with a desperate longing. I kept on running and stretched out my arms, but could not reach him. The distance between us was getting bigger and bigger, and he became smaller and smaller. The rock on which he was standing was carried straight into the sea by a swift tide. The last thing I remember of him was his silhouette with his arms outstretched and the sun blazing behind him.

At the end of our freshman year, only forty students remained out of the original sixty-five. During our second year, the class came under the spell of Dr. Shen, professor of anatomy. Dr. Shen came from a wealthy family and had graduated from the prestigious Shanghai Medical College.

After his postgraduate study in Belgium, where he trained in orthopedic surgery, he returned to China and gave up clinical medicine to teach anatomy in our school.

The Professor had an impressive presence. As a child, he had contracted tuberculosis of the spine which stunted his growth and gave him a disproportionately large head. But he carried himself extremely well and walked with only a slight limp. He was always meticulously dressed in white starched shirts and Western suits, and spoke exact English. His lectures were rapid and intense and he gave us a lot of homework to do. We had to spend many late nights memorizing the trivial details of human anatomy.

To pass anatomy, students had to meet a strict set of standards: they had to show external signs of intelligence, poise and stamina in keeping with the profession; they had to display a certain artistic ability in their anatomical sketches; and of course they had to earn good grades. The Professor was feared as well as revered, since failing anatomy meant failing medical school. He ended up failing half of the class.

Two of the men whom Dr. Shen failed became Communist cadres and came back to haunt him during the Cultural Revolution. They connived with an assistant professor to evict Dr. Shen from his post, and condemned him to hard labor. He had to push carloads of stones and gravel despite his physical disability.

During our third year, the major hurtle was physiology. As our school did not have a physiology professor, the administration had invited a renowned physiologist from Nanjing University to teach the course. Unlike Dr. Shen, our physiology professor Dr. Wu was an amiable person and a dynamic lecturer.

On the first day of class, Dr. Wu made the following announcement: "Those of you who have eaten garlic, please sit in the back row, I positively cannot stand the odor."

Garlic is to Shandong people what hot pepper is to Hunan people. They like to eat raw garlic and raw green onions dipped in a bean sauce and rolled up in a pancake. Raw garlic eaters exude a certain smell; the aroma seems to circulate through their bodies and emanate from their pores.

During our laboratory sessions, we took out the intestines of frogs, put them in a warm saline bath and observed the peristalsis (involuntary contraction). We took out skeletal muscles, and applied an electric current to produce the contraction. On our last day in class, a lamb was bought in and put on the operating table. After anesthetizing the lamb by ether inhalation, the Professor opened its chest and showed us the beating heart, the synchronization of heart and lung, and their response to injected drugs. It was a great inspiration and a relief to finally know that the study of medicine was more than just the memorization of Latin names.

The following day, our class had a farewell party for Dr. Wu, who was to return to Nanjing. The students had prepared a picnic lunch in Seaside Park. The main course of the picnic was braised lamb, accompanied by Viennese bread from a German bakery near the campus. I had never liked lamb, and this one had a peculiar musty taste to it. At the time, I thought it was because they had omitted the garlic, since the Professor disliked it so much. But I loved the crusty bread.

Four decades later, I chanced to meet a man who was president of a medical institution in Beijing. He turned out to be my classmate in medical school, and had served as teaching assistant to Professor Wu. He had bought the lamb from the farmer's market and cared for it before it was put on the operating table. After the lab demonstration, he had carried the carcass to the kitchen, crying all the way. No wonder the lamb had a funny taste.

Class picture of the first post-war graduating class of Shandong University, Medical School, taken on the day before Professor Wu's return to Nanjing. Front row, from the left, two assistant professors, Prof. Shen, Prof. Wu, a professor of biochemistry and Prof Li, Dean of the College. Mei was second to the left in the middle row. 1948.

Chapter 8

EXODUS

When I was a young woman of eighteen, I only had two thing in mind: family and study. The country may have been falling apart around me, but I was oblivious to the political turmoil. During the late 1940s, China was prevented from a post-war recovery by a raging civil war. The Nationalist government devastated after eight years of war with Japan, had failed to improve the lot of common people. Inflation was sky-rocketing and government officials engaged in rampant corruption. Widespread unemployment, poverty and hunger led to increasing social unrest. The public was disillusioned and lost trust in Chiang Kai-shek's government.

Dissatisfaction was particularly strong among intellectuals and college students. During 1947, my second year in college, anti-hunger, anti-war, anti-government and anti-America propaganda was escalating. The number of leftist students grew rapidly. The medical school was located a mile away from the main campus and was at first insulated from the source of political dissent. The faculty and students had, for the most part, decided to keep out of politics, and classes went on as usual. But eventually, the medical school was also caught in the turmoil; several students with presumed Communist connections were arrested.

Once again, Father's face showed the same kind of worry as it had during the height of the Sino-Japanese War. He became preoccupied, and in the evenings, would retire to his favorite chair and brood. In 1948, the Communist army routed the Nationalist forces in Manchuria and threatened Beijing. Officials and civilians with means were plotting their escape. The richest and most influential Chinese fled to America. Other wealthy people chose to go to Hong Kong; those who were not so wealthy but who had government connections went to Taiwan. The great majority of citizens, however, were resigned to their fate. After spending a great part of their lives fleeing the war, and with displacement and family separation still fresh in their minds, they had neither the will nor the means to move.

My father could have asked for a transfer to Taiwan as some of his colleagues had done, but he opted to go to Xiamen (formerly Amoy), the major seaport in Fujian Province, separated from Taiwan by a 200-mile-wide strait. He wanted to adopt a wait-and-see attitude. Lan was to continue her studies as a chemistry major at Xiamen University. I alone had to stay behind because Xiamen University did not have a medical school. My parents were resigned and left me in Qingdao to fend for myself. I moved into the dormitory and for the first time felt the acute pain of separation from my family.

The Communist forces were heading to a swift victory. In the winter of 1948, the Nationalists sued for peace and Chiang Kai-shek briefly resigned as Head of the government. However, in April 1949, the peace talks broke down, and the Communists resumed their military campaign. During the following month, a succession of key cities: Nanjing, Hangzhou, Wuhan and Shanghai, fell to Communist forces, often without a fight.

The atmosphere throughout the university campus was a mixture of fear and resignation. Every few days, Nationalist secret police would raid the dormitories and arrest leftist students. On the surface, people were careful not to align themselves with the leftists. But deep down, everyone knew that it would only be a matter of time until the whole country would be taken over by the Communists. Rumors had it that the underground Communists had black-listed people whom they considered to be Nationalist spies and sympathizers. These people were targeted for punishment once the Communists took power. Most people, particularly those quick to take advantage of the situation, began to veer to the left.

At this point, I began to notice that my classmates were avoiding me as if I had contracted a fatal contagious disease. As time went by, I began to suspect that my casual disapproving remarks of the Communist regime had caused me to be labeled as anti-Communist. It didn't help at all that I had made friends with several veterans of the Nationalist Youth Army Corp, who were fiercely loyal to Chiang Kai-shek. I also worried that I could be punished for having an upper-class family background and for the fact that we had once fled from Communist-occupied territory.

I was constantly plagued by gut-wrenching fear. Memories of struggle meetings were still fresh in my mind. I desperately wanted to get away, but there was nowhere to go, and no one I could even talk to.

Then, unexpectedly, I received a letter from my father who instructed me to go immediately to see his colleague Mr. Liu in the Customs House where he used to work. Mr. Liu, in his late thirties, told me that in a few days he and his family were to be officially transferred to Taiwan. My father had written to him asking him to take me along by claiming me as his dependent younger sister. Circumstances permitting, my father said, the family might join me in Taiwan.

In the same letter, Father had enclosed a letter of introduction and instructed me to take it to his old friend Zhang Xiaoliu who lives in Taiwan.

On the day of departure, I packed my belongings in a small suitcase and told my roommates I was going home. At the pier, I met Mr. Liu, his wife and two young daughters before boarding the ship with them. The small vessel was filled to capacity. After settling in our cabin, I went out on the deck to take a last look at Qingdao. Under the morning sun, I could see a road snaking up and down the coastline and leading to the university hill. Along the way there were sandy beaches, rugged cliffs, little pagodas and an aquarium. It was heart wrenching to think that I might never see this lovely city again.

As the ship moved out of the harbor into the open sea, I was seized by a violent bout of seasickness and was confined to my bed. I was only conscious of the sound of rushing sea waves and the cabin spinning around me. I lost track of time and my thoughts revolved around the family I left behind.

When the ship finally stopped tossing, I emerged from my cabin feeling dizzy and weak. The ship was anchored at Keelung harbor on Taiwan's northern shore. Standing on the deck, in the warm tropical breeze, I felt like I had landed in a foreign country. Throughout much of Chinese history, the Han people on the Chinese mainland had regarded Taiwan as a far-flung outpost inhabited by "barbarians" (of Malay-Polynesian origin) and visited only by Chinese fishermen, smugglers and pirates. During the seventeenth century, various foreign powers: Portuguese, Spanish, British and Dutch, had attempted to settle on the island, but were driven out by one another or by Chinese patriots. After Taiwan was ceded to Japan in the aftermath of the first Sino-Japanese war, the island was largely erased from the Chinese consciousness. Now, with the mainland threatened by the

Communists, Taiwan had become a haven for the members and sympathizers of the Nationalist government.

I waited with the Liu family on board until officials from the Customs House came and whisked us off the boat. As I walked down the plank, a small suitcase in hand, I felt frightened and lost. It was the very first time in my life I was embarking on an adventure without Lan by my side.

The Liu family were placed on a van and taken to their new home in Taipei. I found my way to the City Hall and handed over my father's letter to Mr. Zhang Xiaoliu, chief of staff to the Mayor of Keelung. The letter said:

> *"Honorable brother Xiaoliu:*
>
> *It has been many long years since we last communicated with each other. I have often thought of you and hope that everything has gone well in your life. Now I have a favor to ask of you. My humble daughter Hsiang Mei will be going to medical school in Taiwan. You are the only friend I have on the island and I hope you can give her much needed assistance. My family is currently living in Xiamen. We may have a chance to come to Taiwan soon.*
>
> *I wish you good health and prosperity.*
>
> *Your humble brother, Liu Shendong"*

Mr. Zhang was in his mid-forties, about the same age as my mother, with a dark complexion and of slight build. His eyes were listless, but his movements and speech were swift. I had a strange feeling of deja vu when we talked in our native tongue, a dialect spoken only in our hometown of Lixian in northern Hunan Province. He asked me a few questions about my family just to make sure I was not an imposter. (During the confusion when the Nationalists withdrew from the mainland, many Communists spies were trying to infiltrate

Taiwan. Eventually they were identified, and imprisoned or killed. Their sponsors were severely punished as well, and some were sent to jail).

Mr. Zhang asked me if I had a place to stay. I said, no. He asked me if I had any money to pay for a hotel. I again said, no. Immediately Mr. Zhang took me under his wing. He got permission from the Mayor of the city to put me up in the employees' dormitory where I was to share a room with a woman secretary and have meals in the common dining room. Almost everyone in that dormitory was from Hunan province. The mayor, surnamed Xie, I learned, was also a Hunanese.

I lived in the city employees' dormitory in Keelung for two weeks before Mr. Zhang arranged for a summer job for me teaching Mandarin to local children in a grammar school. The government, which was controlled by Chinese from the mainland, was attempting to erase any Japanese influence through the introduction of Chinese culture and the Mandarin language in schools. Mandarin-speaking teachers were in great demand. I moved into the school and shared a room with several other female teachers who also came from Shandong. It was a great relief to know that I could easily make a living in this time of turmoil.

It struck me as odd that Mr. Zhang would go out of his way to help me, the daughter of an old friend he had not seen in decades. It bothered me to the point that one day I ventured to ask him this question:

"Uncle Zhang, are you and my father very close friends?"

Uncle Zhang was caught by surprise, since Chinese children were not supposed to ask questions. He hesitated for a moment and said: "In fact, I do not know your father."

Seeing the surprise on my face, he added: "I was close to— eh—your mother's side of the family—your grandfather—." He averted his eyes and did not want to say more. To a twenty-year-old girl full of romantic ideas, that could only mean one thing: he was in love with my mother. He probably looked upon me as the daughter he might have had.

By June 1949, seven thousand students who had congregated in Guangzhou were evacuated by boat to Taiwan. In October of 1949, the Nationalist army withdrew from Guangzhou and Xiamen, the last gateways to Taiwan. Just before Xiamen fell, I received a letter from my father saying that the family had no plans to go any place. At that point in time, no one could have predicted that Taiwan was to remain a free and prosperous land.

In the years to come, I realized that it was a combination of luck, my father's resourcefulness, and the help of my parents' old friends that had saved my life. After the liberation, people on the mainland who had previous connections with the Nationalists were severely penalized. The Dean of Shandong University, an appointee of the Nationalist government, had chosen to stay instead of going to Taiwan. He was tried and found guilty by the leftist students. They put him into a sack, tied a rock to it and threw him into the sea.

From the moment I set foot on Taiwan, the strangeness of the place hit me full force. The faces of the people were familiar, but I could neither understand their language nor their thoughts and culture. During the fifty years of Japanese rule, Taiwan had fully integrated Japanese institutions into its traditional Fujian culture.

The long-term goal of finishing medical school was always on my mind. But the most pressing issue was to survive and find a place to live. Like a mountain climber, I had to concentrate on what was immediately ahead, advancing cautiously, one step at a time, and reminding myself not to panic or to think too far ahead. Thus, I faced the challenges with trepidation mixed with a sense of adventure.

When my summer teaching job ended, I went to Taipei to look for a place to live so I could make plans to go back to medical school. But the city was bulging at the seams with refugees and there was no shelter for women. By a streak of luck and with the help of old schoolmates, I found a place to live on the grounds of Taiwan University. It was not a regular dormitory though, or anything close to it. I was allowed to camp out in one of two huts used for storing equipment on the university's athletic field.

The tool shed at the athletic field of Taiwan University where Mei took refuge during the summer of 1949.

GRANDFATHER'S MICROSCOPE

The university was located in what was then a rural area. It was surrounded by woods and cornfields. At night, the athletic field was pitch dark and totally deserted. Somehow, I was never afraid, because crime was virtually unheard of at the time. The Taiwanese had been trained by their Japanese colonial masters to be law-abiding citizens.

The hut was about six feet by ten feet, with a concrete floor, a small window and a sheet of corrugated tin for a roof. Along the walls were two narrow beds, each made of two wooden planks mounted on saw horses. One of the beds served nicely as a multi-purpose table where I set a small propane stove and a wash basin on one side, leaving a space for writing and studying on the other. I had nearly everything I needed, including a public toilet that stood twenty feet away and a little stream running alongside the athletic field. In the morning, I would go to the stream and get a pail of what appeared to be clean water for washing and cooking. One evening while I was out for a walk, I saw a woman standing in the stream washing a chamber pot with a brush. After that I would boil the water before using it to wash my face and brush my teeth. It's a wonder that I did not catch some epidemic diseases such as parasites or hepatitis.

Several times that summer, the island was hit by typhoons. When I heard the first storm warning, I was unperturbed. I had no idea of the power of a typhoon. Besides, there was no place to go to escape it. For two days, the gale blasted across the open field. The wind shook the hut and rain pounded on the tin roof. I was trapped inside, completely unprepared. The only food I had was a bunch of bananas, the cheapest food one could buy. On the second night, I was awakened by a loud metal clang overhead. The wind had torn off the tin roof. I sat up all night in bed as torrential rain pelted down. The next morning, the typhoon finally passed. Some friends helped to put the roof back on and weighed it down with bricks.

Shortly afterwards, I became ill with a spiking high fever and severe weakness. For an entire week, I lay on my cot totally drained of energy. The heat from the tin roof beating down on my body made me drowsy. I was barely conscious.

I felt a warm hand on my forehead.

"Ma?" I asked, not yet awake.

"Little Mei, it's me!" My girl friend Hui's face came into focus. "You must be dreaming!"

I thought I was lying in a bed across from my mother in my childhood home! As a child, I used to will myself to get sick so I could sleep in Mother's room and have food, carefully prepared by Lin Ma, brought to the bedside. The old folks prohibited sick people from eating or drinking anything cold, raw (including fruits), or greasy. The sick would have congee (rice gruel) cooked in chicken broth, and savory egg custard steamed in a bowl with small lean pork meat balls floating on top. But my favorites were snacks of sweet sponge cakes, candies and cookies. The errand boy would be sent running to summon Dr. Zhang. The doctor would arrive in a rickshaw, take my pulse and temperature and dispense a few aspirin. Then they would pile up layers of quilts on top of me until I woke up at night drenched in sweat.

Our parents always remained vigilant against any childhood illnesses. That's why nine of their ten children survived into adulthood.

Hui, my classmate, had stopped by to give me a schedule of the medical school exam that was to take place in two weeks. She boiled water for me to drink and went out and got bread. "It's just a flu, you'll be fine in a few days," she assured me. Hui was one of those lucky people who had a family and a home. Her father was an army officer and they lived in a modest governmental housing compound.

We were both pre-meds, and had not yet studied clinical medicine. But I knew it was not just a flu; there were no respiratory or gastrointestinal symptoms, and no pain anywhere. My urine was the color of milk. I knew I should see a doctor, but I had little money. For the very first time in my life, I realized that I was not invincible. I thought to myself: "Here I am, lying in this little hut just across the strait from my family. I could die in here and they would not even know it."

I thought of Blackie, the family dog we left behind when we fled Weihai and Communism. Now I am just like her, abandoned and left to die alone. The thought made me so sad that I could not stop weeping. At a time when death and human tragedies were commonplace, one human life seemed as trivial as an ant on the ground. The prospect of a long and difficult road ahead made me cringe and drained the hope and energy out of me.

As I lay in bed at night, a beam of light fell on my face. I looked up and saw a cloudless sky and a full moon framed in my little window. The sight of that softly glowing disk brought to mind a poem my mother taught me when I was a child. "Thoughts on a Tranquil Night" by Li Po, a famous poet of the Tang dynasty (A.D. 701-762)

> Before my bed a pool of light,
> Is it hoarfrost upon the ground?
> Eyes raised, I see the moon so bright;
> Head bent, in homesickness I'm drowned.
>
> (Translated by Xu Yuan-Zhong in
> "300 Tang Poems, a New Translation."
> The Commercial Press, Hong Kong)

The poem had been a favorite among children because of its simplicity and nice rhyme. Now, I finally understood the meaning packed in those concise, elegant words. The poem connected me to the summer nights when the whole family would sit around the court yard to watch the moon and catch the cool breeze. The air was pungent from the burning of the herbal mosquito coils. The adults would fan themselves with large banana-leaf fans and tell stories.

On the night of the moon festival on the 15th day of the eighth lunar month, when the moon was at its fullest and most brilliant, we would eat moon cakes and drink tea, and listen to the tales of the moon fairy and the hare. That night I would try to stay awake to catch a glimpse of the beautiful fairy when she stepped out of the moon. It was said that whoever caught sight of the fairy could have his/her wish granted. Of course I never stayed awake long enough to see her.

Those days, our only amusement was to make music, which we did with passion. Lan and I taught ourselves to play harmonica, and we played duets for our parents and siblings. Then we sang the songs we learned in school and in the movies. Our grand finale was always a song called "My Happy Family." My father was proud that he had enough children to form a musical band, a basketball team or even a small army.

Of course, ill and homesick, I only remembered the happy times. The fights, the tension, and the resentment of the old days were all forgotten. The jealousy and hatred I had for my first aunt vanished. If she were to appear in front of me, I would have embraced her and wept with joy. It may have been a dysfunctional family, but still deep down I knew that we all cared for one another. They pinned so many hopes on me, giving me the best possible care and education. I was now the only one left in the free world. I decided that I would not let them down.

Hui brought fruit to me and cooked rice gruel on the kerosene stove every day. One of her friends who was working as an apprentice in an army hospital pharmacy brought along a fistful of white pills. He said they were some kind of anti-infectious tablets. They looked very much like the ones that had cured Lan's dysentery. So I took the pills, and the fever gradually abated. Within two weeks, my health returned and my intense homesickness began to subside.

In the fall, I was accepted by Taiwan University Medical School. I was thrilled; it was my dream come true. I moved into a spacious room which I shared with two other female students. After months in the leaky hut, it felt like indescribable luxury. I was immensely grateful to the Nationalist government for providing me with a scholarship that paid tuition, room and board in exchange for a few hours' work in the library. Still, I was plagued with a lot of uncertainties about the immediate future of Taiwan and about the fate of my family in China. Not the least of my worries was the language barrier.

During my childhood when my family had moved around the country, we children had learned to quickly pick up dialects. Within six months of arriving at a new place, we would be able to speak like natives. At the university though, Lan and I had abandoned the local dialects, choosing instead to speak the official language of Mandarin. We had heard it spoken by our parents, teachers, and friends, but it was our love of Peking opera that made us perfect the dialect.

The ordinary people in Taiwan spoke the *min nan* (southern Fujian Province) dialect which is unlike any of the dialects I had known. And the educated elite spoke only Japanese. Now I began to have regrets about not taking the opportunity to learn Japanese while our family lived under Japanese occupation.

Out of 102 students in our class, approximately ten percent were mainlanders who had come from medical schools all over China. Some had come with their families who were officials or employees of the Nationalist government, and a handful of us were on our own. The mainlanders tended to stick together because of our common language and cultural background. The local students treated us with Japanese-style courtesy. But I could not help wondering whether underneath all that civility, they looked upon us as intruders or even enemies. It was easy to imagine the anger and frustration of the Taiwanese doctors who were taught by Japanese mentors and had felt secure and comfortable as Japanese citizens. After the Japanese withdrawal, they were left to deal with a new set of authorities, a different language, culture, political regime and an uncertain future.

The Nationalist government had banned Japanese as an official language. In private, though, the doctors and medical students continued to converse in Japanese, interspersed with German medical terminology. In classes, the professors would attempt to lecture in Mandarin, but the result was often a jumble of bad Mandarin, equally bad Taiwanese dialect and broken English. Sometimes the only thing I got out of the lectures were the names of the diseases written in English on the blackboard. When my patience wore thin, I would sneak out of the back door of the auditorium and take walks in the nearby New Park. In the evenings, I would go to the library and study English textbooks. My habit of self study, which began in high school during the Communist occupation, again paid off. I managed to get good grades and graduated at the very top of my class.

At this point, several students were enticed to join the Nationalist Party. We were responding to a propaganda campaign spearheaded by Chiang Ching-kuo, son and heir of President Chiang Kai-shek. The government had learned a bitter lesson for having neglected the student movement on the mainland, which had contributed significantly to the downfall of the regime. To rally student support, Chiang Ching-kuo established an intercollegiate organization, the Chinese Anti-Communist National Salvation Youth Corp. Its goal was to indoctrinate students with the official ideology of the ruling party, called the "Three People's Principles:" People's sovereignty (Nationalism), People's rights (Democracy), and People's Livelihood (Socialism).

GRANDFATHER'S MICROSCOPE

When I attended my first Nationalist Party meeting, I was expecting to see a pompous official full of political mumbo jumbo, preaching the holy war of restoration of the Nationalist control of the mainland. Instead, there was this scholarly young man who spoke with enthusiasm and sincerity about the measures the government was undertaking to improve the lot of the common people, especially the poor on the island.

The most surprising thing I heard was the government's new land reform program, which was meant to eliminate exploitation of poor tenant farmers. The government sold public land acquired from the Japanese to the tenant farmers at low prices, and in a "land to the tiller program," limited the amount of land each landlord could own.

For a moment, I thought I had gone to the wrong meeting, the Communists' meeting. In the end, I saw no great difference in the basic goals between the Nationalist and the Communist parties. (Both Chiang Kai-shek and Chiang Ching-kuo had gone to school in the Soviet Union. The younger Chiang was at one time a devout Communist).

As it turned out, the well-planned and well-executed land reform program was a stunning success. The production of rice doubled in a few years, both farmers and the government reaped huge gains. It reversed the economical downturn and paved the way for agricultural and industrial progress that eventually led to the "Taiwan Miracle." It seemed ironic to me that the Nationalist party was the one that could achieve a socialist goal, and without resorting to violence and cruelty, as the Communists had.

During the last year of medical school, half of the mainlanders in my class were planning to go to the U.S. or Europe. The most obvious reason was that we wanted to get the best medical training possible, and lucky for us, there was a shortage of doctors in the U.S. The other reason was that, deep in my heart, I did not feel at home in Taiwan, and I could not see a future for myself in that environment. Also,

I felt I stood a better chance of seeing my family again if I left.

At the time, the tension between mainland China and Taiwan was like a bomb ready to explode. The Chinese Communists hated the U.S. with a passion for helping Taiwan. That's why I had to keep my whereabouts a secret for fear of bringing trouble to my family. I would write letters with cryptic messages to a friend in Hong Kong who would then re-post my letters to my family so that it would seem that I was living in Hong Kong. This was the letter I wrote before leaving for the States:

> *Venerable Father and Mother:*
>
> *Since my graduation from medical school, I have wanted to get advanced training in medicine at a big hospital, in the place where the people in the oil portrait came from. Now my wish is granted and I will soon embark on this journey. Don't worry about me, everything is going well. I am healthy in body and in spirit. I will write again when I arrive at the new hospital. Wishing you good health,*
>
> *Daughter Mei*

I borrowed money from friends and bought a third-class passenger ticket on the S.S. President Wilson. It was smooth sailing in the Pacific Ocean, but a severe case of seasickness confined me to the upper bunk bed in the third class cabin. I survived on orange juice and crackers brought to my bed. During the nineteen days aboard the ship, I passed the time worrying about my family in China. How were they coping with life under Communism? Would my father be without a job again? How could he feed the family?

As I lay on my bed trying to command my mind to swing along with the boat, I had a sense of deja vu. My thought went back to the time when I was sailing out of China with my future in the balance. Now, in just four years, I had become a doctor, and about to embark on an exciting career in a country where dreams come true. My brain told me that I should be elated, but my heart was heavy with worry and uncertainty. I knew nothing about America, just images from the movie screen. How could I fit in among these beautiful, rich, singing and dancing people?

Friends told me not to worry, we Chinese had always done well everywhere in the world, but still I felt naive and unprepared. I knew from medical school that it would take an entire lifetime just to master the craft. And what about a new language, a new culture, a new way of living and behaving? How long would it take to learn? How could I measure up to the graduates of Harvard and Yale who were already light years ahead of me?

To spend nineteen days aboard the ship was like an eternity. I was so relieved to have finally set my foot on solid ground in San Francisco and to begin the next exciting chapter of my life.

Chapter 9

My ABC Daughter

Pamela Wang Anderson (1st daughter)

Thanksgiving

When I was a little girl, the toughest holiday for me was Thanksgiving.

Holidays were confusing times for my mother. Most American holidays are Christian holidays, or American patriotic holidays and my mother was unfamiliar with them. Luckily, I didn't have to do too much explaining about Christian holidays, since she had been liberally exposed to Christian missionaries in China, and was now totally uninterested in religious holidays.

But she was also uninformed about American holidays. When I would bring home my latest masterpiece from school (for example, a picture of an American flag), she would happily display it as evidence of my artistic prowess. But when asked to explain what it was to a Chinese friend, she would mumble, "Oh, something from her school; something American, like that."

But Thanksgiving was always the hardest holiday. It was because of Thanksgiving that I knew my family wasn't normal.

Being the first child of immigrant parents, I learned about how to be an American in school and in Girl Scouts. In school, I learned how to speak and write like an American. Girl Scouts taught me how to think and act like an American. Between the two of them, I learned what was right, what was wrong, what to like and what to dislike. However, this learning was definitely a double-edged sword. Once in the know, I spent much of my life being embarrassed by my mother's appearance, her behavior and her speech, since she was clearly not an American.

School, the source of social correctness, taught me that Thanksgiving was a time that families came together. Even if the members didn't live together, they made a special effort to meet on Thanksgiving and eat turkey. In school, we also learned that a normal family has a certain structure. There are, of course, parents (a mother and a father). There must also be children, usually two, a boy and a girl. But there are also other necessary members of the normal family, such as grandparents (2 sets), aunts and uncles (several) and cousins (many). Then there are the less well-explained relationships, such as the "second cousin twice removed." As the sixties wore on, and our family acquired a television, I also learned, through watching shows like "Leave it to Beaver," and "The Donna Reed Show," what a real American family looked like. It didn't look like our family.

In our family, there was only a mother, a father and children. As each Thanksgiving rolled around, the hole in our family tree bothered me more and more. The other members were never spoken of, in fact, I wasn't sure there were other members. I tried to think whether it was possible that Mother and Father didn't have parents, but that thought taxed the limit of my understanding of reproduction. As youngsters do not tolerate brooding well, I brought this issue to my mother's attention just before Thanksgiving.

"How come everyone has grandparents and I don't?" I asked one day.

"Of course you have grandparents, they're just not here," my mother answered, somewhat taken aback.

"But why can't we ever see them? Are they hiding? Why don't they visit us at Thanksgiving?" I couldn't ask what I was really thinking, which was, why didn't they love us and visit us?

"Well, of course they're not hiding. Don't be silly. Go play now." This was my mother's ultimate explanation and I knew from experience that more was not forthcoming.

Since I wasn't sure what I was missing by not having grandparents, I did some detective work to determine whether they were worth having. Most of my classmates, when questioned about what their grandparents were like, made faces and said things like: "Yechh. They hug you and kiss you and make you play the piano. And they have hair in their ears and smell like mothballs."

One year, as Thanksgiving approached, I somehow got it into my head that my real grandparents had decided to surprise us and come for Thanksgiving dinner. Perhaps I veered a little too close to the edge of reality that fall, because for the first time, my mother decided to be a normal mother and cook a turkey for Thanksgiving.

My mother was idea-free about why an entire nation, who had invented the atom bomb and the toaster, would want to collectively eat turkey on a given day in November. The meat was rubbery and tasteless! And the accompaniments, such as stuffing, mashed potatoes and pies; well, it was difficult for her to understand how anyone would want to eat this food. And so, for Thanksgiving, we had Peking duck instead.

But that year, I had managed to convince my mother to prepare a turkey. I was sure that it was the magic ingredient needed to make my grandparents appear. I was on pins and needles the day of the big feast, wondering when and how they would appear. Would they ring the doorbell before the meal and sweep in the door in the midst of "Ay-yahs!" galore, or would they sneak in the back door when we were sitting down to rubbery turkey and surprise us while we were eating? I tried to imagine what they would say about me, their only grandchild, but could only come up with lots of "Ay-yahs!", and the smell of mothballs. I started diligently practicing the piano.

Long after the dinner was eaten, my mother found me crying on the floor of my closet. "What's wrong?" she asked tenderly.

I stuttered out the whole thing to her, somehow deeply ashamed at my wish that my grandparents would come and visit me.

"Someday you will see them, but not now." She said with a grim face.

That's why, for me, Thanksgiving is still the hardest holiday. It is a reminder of what I don't have. Nowadays, I always make more turkey than I need, maybe in hopes that unexpected guests will drop in. But they never do. And why should they? I don't think they like turkey.

Family, American-style

Although I never knew my real grandparents, I did have some grandparents, American-style.

When my mother arrived in America, she was a young, pretty, naïve, lonely woman. And she was pregnant. In short, she was an irresistible sight for an older woman in search of someone to mother. She quickly accumulated a few sets of foster parents.

One set was Burton and Maud Hayes, an elderly couple who were introduced to my mother by a Lebanese nurse at the hospital. Mr. Hayes was a high school teacher and Mrs.

Hayes stayed home. To my mother, who thinks of people as "social friends" or "true friends," the Hayes' were true friends. The one little problem was that they were also devout Christians who saw in Mother an opportunity to bring a heathen into the fold. After a lot of talking, they arranged for her to come with them to church. Since Mother only had one good dress, the universal female problem of what to wear was automatically solved. So, when the Hayes' arrived one fine Sunday morning to pick her up, the sight that greeted them was my mother in her one and only dress: a skin-tight, black lace Mandarin gown, slit up to mid-thigh on either side.

"Praise the lord!" shouted Grandpa Hayes, when he saw her.

Grandma Hayes was unperturbed. After all, a soul was at stake; no time to get upset about fashion trends. She beckoned my mother into the car and off they went.

Mother eventually discerned that black lace, thigh-baring dresses were not the best church garments. She looked around at what people were wearing and then bought some gray corduroy fabric from which she made a jumper that became her "church dress." Eventually, she solved the fashion problem altogether by ceasing to go to church.

Granny Marsden was the foster grandmother I came to know best. After I was born, I stayed for a time with my mother in the women doctor and nurses' dormitory. But that didn't work out very well. Mother had to leave me alone for long periods of time and I was always crying, which was terrible for the nurses, who were trying to get some sleep. While they were fond of me, my constant crying didn't prevent them from fervently wishing to see my backside exiting the building. Granny Marsden lived across the street from the hospital where my mother worked. She had a grandchild almost exactly my age that she was caring for during the day while her daughter worked. Somehow, she heard from Sophie, the gossipy old housekeeper at the hospital about my mother's (and the nurses') plight and I suppose she thought that if she had to care for one tiny child, why not two? But there was probably more than efficiency at work here; Granny Marsden was a good Christian woman who liked to help others. And she knew my mother was desperate for help.

Granny (her real name was Anna), lived with her husband, Jim, in a modest wooden house across the street from the General Hospital. They were both of German descent, hard-working and uncomplaining. Jim was remarkably taciturn, in fact, I don't actually remember hearing him speak. Granny cared for her granddaughter, Dianne, and me as if we were sisters. But we couldn't have been less alike in appearance and temperament. Dianne was small for her age, quiet, and delicate. I was large for my age, boisterous and prone to trouble. We must have made an interesting sight on our daily walks; Granny Marsden, pushing two strollers down the sidewalk, her gray page boy bobbing gently in the breeze, dressed in her sensible shoes and sensible jumper. In one stroller, a quiet, delicate Caucasian girl, sucking her thumb. In the other, a squealing Chinese girl, kicking at nothing in particular. We became a well-known sight in the neighborhood, but also the topic of major speculation.

Finally, someone couldn't stand it any more and asked Granny's neighbor: "Say, is that Jim a Chinaman or what?"

Many years later, Mother sent Granny Marsden a mink stole for Christmas. Granny, she recollected, had never been wealthy enough to own a mink. Granny was quite surprised by the gesture and got a lot of pleasure out of that gift for many years—in my mind's eye, I see her wearing that mink stole proudly to church-sponsored bingo games. There is no doubt that she was the only lady in the church so grandly attired. When Granny died, Mother said, between her tears, that she was glad that she had sent that mink to her and that she wished she had had more opportunities to pay Granny back for all the good things she had done for us.

When I was eight, two strangers came to our house and stayed a long time. They lived in the tiny den, with its attached bathroom. I was delighted when I found out they were uncles. But, on trying to determine which uncles they were, I got a blank look. Apparently, they weren't "real" uncles, but rather, they were friends of my parents. Inexplicably, they chose to call themselves "uncles." Although at first I was somewhat conflicted, I finally ended up dealing with this genealogical dilemma by calling them "Uncle" at home and referring to them as "family friends" at school. Before long, Uncle Guo, one of the Uncles in the Den promoted himself to "godfather." Luckily for us, he wasn't the Italian kind of godfather.

Uncle Guo and my mother were old friends; they had been schoolmates on the Mainland. One of Uncle Guo's stated goals in coming to visit us, he said, was to improve his English. I used to regularly converse with him to help him attain this goal. Near the end of his visit, he thanked me for helping him to expand his English pronunciation. As an example of his prowess, he demonstrated his mastery of the word "fire."

"I used to think that it was pronounced 'fear,' but now I know it's pronounced 'fare,' " he said proudly.

When I was older, he sent me stamps from Taiwan, which was a delight for me, but for some reason, a burden to my mother. Whenever she got a thick envelope from Uncle Guo stuffed with stamps, she would toss them to me with a sigh, "More stamps! Ay-yah! Waste of money!"

Many years later, when Mother heard that Uncle Guo was sick, she immediately went to visit him in Taiwan, fearing the worst. He was emaciated; a shadow of his former robust self. He knew he was dying. He pressed some gold coins into her hand, "For your children," he whispered. He died shortly thereafter. Since I have nothing in the way of keepsakes from my grandparents, I have come to think of Uncle Guo's gold coin as an important memento. I keep it in a little wooden box on my dresser. Sometimes when I am unhappy or restless, I open the box and look at the coin. Then I think of my Uncle in the Den, young and laughing, hair standing straight up (no matter how much greasy kid-stuff he poured on it, it never laid flat), sleeves of his ironed white dress shirt rolled up, smoking furiously, talking up a storm in Chinese. I'm not sure what he's saying, but Mother used to describe his Chinese vocabulary like this: "Coarse soldier talk! Every other word is a swear word: F this and F that, oh dear, I'm too embarrassed to translate."

That's when I think happily, "That's my Uncle."

My Mother's Microscope

When I was eight, my mother started studying for a big test. She was trying to pass her board (the American Board of Pathology) exam, but I didn't know that at the time. Her studying didn't have too much impact on my life; she was still mom and made dinner and kept the house. But I slowly learned that there was more to her than I had initially realized. She had this whole other life that I didn't know anything about and she spent a lot of time in the den, with her books, studying.

As a child, I used to find her textbooks sinister and eerie. From a child's perspective, they were huge, like the books of Merlin the Wizard in the movies. Also, they had the most forbidding, menacing smell. In retrospect, much of their smell must have come from the chemicals in the pathology lab: formalin, alcohol, xylene. But at the time, to me they smelled like alien mushrooms. To top it off, there were the most horrifying pictures in the books: pictures of pieces of people (without the rest of the people attached), people cut open like chickens, things that looked like dead babies. Definitely, the books were creepy. But there was something else besides the books that she used for her studying that was not creepy; there was a microscope.

Thinking back, it was just a modest, gray, working microscope, nothing fancy. But to me, the microscope was an object worthy of awe. First of all, it was definitely an adult thing. It was very heavy; a real piece of machinery, like the gasoline lawnmower; too big and heavy for a kid to lift. Second, only an adult could look in it and actually see anything. It was one of the clearest demonstrations to me at the time that adult eyes were able to see things that kids' eyes could not. Whenever I peered through the eyepieces, I saw only darkness. Once I thought I saw something, and I got all excited, but it turned out to be just the reflection of my own eye.

As I got older and Mom went back to work, my overwhelming image is of her at her microscope. I remember her perched on a chair, her back straight ("Never slouch at the microscope!" she used to tell me), arching her neck forward to look into the eyepieces, under her elbow a stack of slide trays.

I remember the first time I looked at slides with her. I had just graduated from high school and was working in the histology lab during the summer. We were looking into a teaching microscope, which is a very Star Wars-looking apparatus where several people can look simultaneously at the same slide. My mother was "driving;" that is, she was twisting the knobs to move the slide around underneath the magnifying lens. As her fingers spun the slide expertly, she pointed out the landmarks, sort of like a microscopic tour bus driver. As her fingers kept spinning the slide around, I started feeling a little queasy. A small sweat broke out on my upper lip and I started to regret the large, spicy lunch I had just finished. Luckily, I did not need to avail myself of the trash can at my feet, as the microscopic tour ended shortly thereafter. But I never forgot the expert way my mother twirled the slide and explained for me the structure of the nerve and what the different colors of stains meant. It was as if she was holding the door to an exotic land partly open, enough for me to glimpse the fascinating and privileged world just beyond my grasp. I went to college and worked hard.

During my last year of college, my status as a biology major allowed me to enroll in a year-long histology course. In part I chose histology because of the excellent reputation of the professors. But I also chose it because I wanted to understand better the glimpses through the microscope my mother had given me. I spent the year staring, entranced, at tissues and organs through the little microscopes in the histology lab.

When I got the letter from my future medical school congratulating me on my entry into the class of 1982, they also sent a list of books and equipment I would need in order to start classes. At the top of the list was a compound microscope of a certain style. The letter mentioned how much a new microscope might cost. I stared at that number for a while. It was more money than I had ever spent for one thing in my entire life, including my rusty '70 Pinto. I went to the student bulletin board and found a used one instead. The price of the used scope, while high, was affordable and I was assured by the second-year student that I would be able to sell it the following year for nearly what I paid.

When I slid it out of its box for the first time, I gasped. Somehow, I hadn't expected it to be so beautiful. It was a blonde color with matte black accents. The stage was black and the objectives were shining silver. At that moment, I thought it was the most beautiful thing I had ever seen. It was heavy; I needed to use two hands to extract it from its snug box. I looked at the scope for a long while, thinking. I was finally on the threshold of that narrow door to a privileged world. And my microscope would open the door for me.

Pathology was my favorite class in medical school. The professors were extremely smart and cool. I was fascinated by the appearance of disease. But most of all, it gave me a way to connect with my mother. I would learn about a disease and I would think, "Mom looked at gross specimens just like these when she was in medical school," or "Mom saw slides of this disease when she was a student." Even though our experiences were widely separated in space and time, we shared something similar, my Mother and I. Perhaps it was the only thing that we shared that way in our lives.

When the time came to sell the microscope, I was very sad. But I knew I couldn't afford to keep such a valuable piece of machinery if I wasn't going to use it. I could barely make the rent each month, even with two part-time jobs. I sold it to a first year student who got the same gleam in his eyes as I did when he first saw the microscope. And when I saw that, I knew it was the right thing to do, that he would take care of my microscope and pass it on to someone else who appreciated it.

And I did endure and graduate from medical school, and have somehow made it through each day since then without owning a microscope. But last year, before my 25-year college reunion, I saw a little ad on my school's Web site, "Special deal—old microscopes for sale." I clicked on a button and was connected to a very nice professor in the biology department who informed me that the College was getting new microscopes and that they were disposing of the old ones to interested alumnae willing to make a donation. And I'm not sure why, but I bought a microscope, sight unseen. I keep telling everyone that it was to help out the College, but I don't think that's the reason.

When the scope arrived and I unpacked it, I squeaked with delight. It was perfect. All black and brass and gleaming with a perfect little mirror, a little metal plaque with the school's name and even an old wooden box of plant slides. The nice biology professor included a note assuring me that he had picked the finest of the microscopes for me and polished it himself and picked out the slides, to boot.

Coincidentally, my microscope was made by Leitz, the oldest microscope-maker in Germany and the same company that made my great-grandfather's microscope.

The microscope sits on my bookshelf and every now and then I slide off the plastic cover and turn the mirror to catch the light. I look at the plant slides, smell the histology lab smells in my memory, and think of my other microscope. And finally, in my mind's eye, I see Mother sitting ramrod straight in front of her microscope, a tray of slides at her elbow, lost in the world of pink and purple. And at that moment the microscope becomes more than just an optical instrument; it becomes a time machine, an instrument that brings the past in focus and magnifies all that is good.

Chapter 10

BECOMING A NEUROPATHOLOGIST

When I first started out in pathology, I was assigned a desk space in the histology lab. Sitting next to me was another first-year resident, Joseph, with whom I was to share a microscope. During the entire year, Joe and I never had a regular conversation; we communicated by gestures. I was practically mute, while Joe spoke a rapid Italian mixed with a few English words.

Microscope is the major tool a pathologist uses, and, like an automobile, it's a very personal one as well. A microscope has to be adjusted to fit the user's eyes; it needs regular cleaning, polishing and servicing. A good microscope not only make you see better, it's also a status symbol. The newest and most expensive microscopes would go to the people on the high echelon. As the lowest-ranking house officers, Joe and I shared the oldest microscope in the department. It was a monocular (one-eyed) microscope, rarely used even in those days. And yet, this microscope was the most heavily used one in the department. To avoid conflict, I would go to work at 6.30 in the morning. By the time Joe showed up at 8.30 am, I would be finished with the microscope and ready to do something else: performing an autopsy, attending a conference, or going to the library. I would stay late in the afternoon after everyone else had left, so I could use the microscope.

At the end of the first year, Joe suddenly disappeared, and I was promoted to having my own microscope. When I first peeked into this binocular microscope, I was quite alarmed; there were two separate images in front of my eyes. I felt cross-eyed and dizzy. After days of struggling with the double vision, my brain learned the trick, and suddenly, the two small images merged into a big one. I was on my way to see, through this powerful instrument, the awesome spectacles of the struggle for survival in the human body. I would sit in front of a microscope for hours on end entranced by the architectural perfection of the living tissues. After staining with dyes, the cells lighted up like the stained glass windows in a medieval cathedral. The sight would fill me with a religious feeling and a sense of mystery. Who was the creator of this miracle?

When the organs were attacked by disease, the cells would become alive and speak to me in a secret language. I could see how they react to danger signals and how different cells cooperate to defend the turf. In the wound, blood proteins rapidly solidify into clots to plug the vessels and stop the bleeding. Meanwhile, white blood cells squeeze through the wall of the blood vessels and swarm into the wound to engulf the bacteria; new cells are manufactured to replace the dead ones. I felt awed and privileged to witness, at close range, the miracles of life and death.

In time, I learned to ignore the physical unpleasantness of the autopsies and to concentrate instead on the intellectual challenges and rewards. Using a scalpel and a microscope, I provided answers to the questions posed by the clinical doctors. The cause of death was always their primary concern, but equally important was the fear that they might have missed something or should have done it differently. The autopsy enables the clinicians to see what's taking place inside their patients. That's how they learn and become better doctors, and why the pathologists are regarded as "doctors' doctor."

I had great respect for our chief, Dr. Milton Bohrod who was Jewish, cultivated, and a liberal democrat. He taught us how to think and judge for ourselves instead of believing everything we were told. He was skillful in anatomical dissection, and would say to us: "Work like a surgeon, not a butcher," "Treat the body with respect," "Treat the tissues as if they were jewels."

Dr. Bohrod once told the story that Professor Rudolf Virchow, the German master and founder of pathology, could perform an autopsy without getting one drop of blood on his tuxedo. In time, I was confident that I would not get one drop of blood on my tuxedo had I chosen to wear one.

Of all the human organs, the brain fascinated me the most. The first time I watched a brain being taken out the skull of a dead person, I felt an acute anxiety and pain. Here was the essence of a human being, the repository of his life experiences, intelligence, personality and the very soul. Now it had turned into a white, lifeless mass like tofu. What happened to his thoughts and emotions? Where did his spirit go?

When I told my fellow residents about this awful feeling, one man said: "That didn't bother me. What bothered me most was seeing a patient had his penis cut off because of cancer!"

Autopsy is only a small part of pathology. The most challenging part is surgical pathology: the diagnosis of diseases on biopsy sample taken from live patients. It is a skill that would take me many years to master.

After five years of residency and two years as attending staff, I felt I needed to advance beyond the daily routine of general pathology, and specialize in subjects that I was particularly interested in. That's why I turned down an offer to become director of laboratories at a private hospital and instead spent a year as a research fellow under the tutelage of Dr. Edith Potter, founder of neonatal pathology. It is a subject that has always fascinated me, and deals with embryonic development and diseases of the newborn infants.

My research assignment was to study the development of the human brain and the endocrine system. I studied hundreds of human embryos that were the products of miscarriage at different gestational ages. Each embryo had been made into hundreds of slides by serial section. Using a microscope, I was able to follow, step by the step, the precisely programmed, dynamic and generally flawless development of the human organism. It was fascinating to observe how a sheet of ectodermal cells (skin cells) in a tiny embryo could multiply, fold, twist, expand and finally evolve into the most miraculous of all human organs, the brain.

When Dr. Potter retired, I moved to another department, and resolved to specialize in neuropathology, or diseases of the nervous system, but there was no one to teach me. At the time, neuropathologists were in great demand. Our hospital, like many others in the country, did not have a neuropathologist. I would have to go to New York or Washington for the training, but with a husband and three children, that was not an option. Then I decided to study on my own, learning on the job. Two years later, I passed the specialty board examination and became a board-certified neuropathologist. But it would take me many more years to become fully confident about my diagnostic skill.

* * *

Dr. Liu! You are wanted in surgery, stat!"
"Tell them I'm on my way now," I said.

As I replied to the nurse, I was already jogging down the corridor.

Once again, I reflected ruefully that a busy neuropathologist's life is a lot of running to the neurosurgeon's tune. As a neuropathologist, I used my microscope to tell neurosurgeons what is that thing growing in their patient's head. Even though I was the doctor who was most removed from the patient (most of the time, I never saw the patients), it was my opinion that was the final word upon which the patient's treatment was based.

Although some pathologists were frustrated surgeons, I was not. I was quite content to work in the shadows. I knew I was not surgeon material.

Breathless, I ran into the frozen section room inside the OR suite. A masked circulating nurse was waiting for me and wordlessly handed me a folded green surgical towel. I unfolded the towel, and then carefully opened the damp, white sterile gauze inside. I saw two tiny pieces of brain tissue. Just looking at it, I already knew it was diseased. Unlike normal brain, which was white and homogeneous like tofu, these fragments were greyish and granular. After donning latex gloves, I picked up a small pair of forceps, gently lifted the tissue and placed it inside the cryostat, a frozen section machine, which looked like a small, clear-topped freezer on wheels. Inside, the temperature was rapidly lowered to -25 degrees, freezing the brain tissue within seconds. When frozen hard, I sliced the frozen brain tissue with a razor-sharp blade mounted on the inside of the machine. I then quickly picked up the frozen wafer-thin sections on a glass slide, stained them for a minute with dyes and readied the slide for examination under the microscope.

After ten years, reading frozen sections was not overly stressful. But it wasn't always so. I still remember the panic I felt as a young pathologist, trying to come up with the right diagnosis while looking at a tiny snippet of crushed and distorted tissue. The patient lay unconscious with a hole in his head, surgeons and nurses, standing patiently around, hands wrapped in sterile towels. There's no time to dwell on the differential diagnoses, or to consult colleagues and books. You just have to come up with the right answer from the top of your head. When there is the slightest doubt about the diagnosis, you must have the humility to admit that you don't know. Tell the surgeon to close up, you need more time. On rare occasions, it may take days of study, special tests, discussions and consultations before you can make up your mind.

The consequences of a wrong diagnosis are devastating. If a patient had a malignancy that was missed by the pathologist, the result is, of course, fatal, and if a false malignancy was reported, the patient could be subjected to unnecessary mutilating surgery such as removal of part of a brain, a lung, a breast, or a limb. Even after many years in the business, I still feel a sort of uneasiness, an apprehension each time I walk into the OR, like a performer going on stage. There may well be a bizarre case I have never seen before, and I know perfectly well that even the best of us have made mistakes.

What I saw under the microscope confirmed my suspicions. I dialed a number and was connected to the room where the craniotomy was taking place.

"Dr. Silver, this is Dr. Liu. I have the pathological diagnosis on Carol Walker, it is a medulloblastoma," I said in my most neutral tone of voice.

"Thank you," said the surgeon. This was bad news for the child. In fact, it was a death sentence. I stayed behind for a few minutes, cleaning up the cryostat and dictating my pathological report into the machine in the room. I then headed back to my office, to finish my day's work. As I walked out of the OR suite, I passed by the relative's waiting room. I saw Dr. Silver sitting there, his arm around a young blonde woman, her face buried in her hands, her shoulders heaving silently. My eyes locked with those of the gentle-looking young man who was standing over his wife. His eyes were full of agony. It was their child on whom I had pronounced the death sentence of medulloblastoma. I had seen that agony before. I could not meet his gaze.

Hastily I walked down the corridors, fixing my eyes on the floor. When I got to my office, I closed the door, sat down at my desk, and let the tears flow.

❋ ❋ ❋

It was one scorching 95 degree summer day in Taiwan in 1952. The operating room was tightly closed to keep away the draft and germs, and there was no air conditioning. After I had put on a mask, a cap, a scrub suit and, on top of that, a long-sleeved surgical gown, I began to perspire. The patient was an eight-year-old girl whose nasal sinuses were filled with a massive tumor that had recurred despite previous surgeries. The ENT surgeon had to open up her nose and scrape out the tumor bit by bit. As the lowest ranking member of the team, my job was to hold the retractors. The child was not given general anesthesia, since they could not put a mask over her face. In those days, the doctors were not experienced with IV administered anesthetics and they had to resort to local injections of novocaine to numb the pain. The child was conscious and screaming for her mom the whole time.

Two hours into the surgery, I was weak and perspiring profusely from heat and hunger. Three hours earlier I had a typical dormitory breakfast, which consisted of a bowl of rice gruel and a few strands of leafy vegetables. I had not taken in a lot of water for fear that I might have to go to the bathroom in the midst of a surgery. On top of it all, I was totally unnerved by the child's hoarse cry of pain and fear. The idea that I had to hold steady and not move a muscle for God only knew how long created in me a panic attack. I feared I was not going to make it through. My heart started to race, my hands were shaking and I felt nauseated. Fearing that I might throw up on the operating table, I blurted out in a weak voice: "I can't go on any more."

Then came a muffled order from the surgeon, a forty-year-old, dark and burly man. "You can not leave!"

A few more moments passed, I was losing my sight, the bloodstained green towel became a blur and my hands lost their grip on the retractors. I turned around, staggered a few steps and collapsed onto the floor. The surgery continued in total silence. I did not know how long I sat on the floor with my head between my knees. Eventually, I regained my sight and the use of my legs. I went to the locker room, changed into my street clothes and walked out into the corridor. There I saw a young woman, mother of the patient, standing by the window. She was covering her face with a handkerchief, sobbing and shaking; she had heard her child's screams.

My heart immediately broke. I was overcome with an immense guilt and a sense of helplessness. This patient reminded me of my childhood friend Liu Ming who had died of a nasopharyngeal tumor. I wanted to put my arm around the young mother and comfort her, but I had not seen other doctors doing it. So I walked on. The lesson I learned during that year was that you have to be made of iron, body and soul, to be a surgeon.

My youngest half-sister, Mang, died in 1948 when she was only three years old. Always a delicate child, she had developed a lot of boils on her scalp. These were treated with topical application of *gaoyao*, a large square band-aid with a black tar-like herbal medicine. It didn't help. She looked ill and listless. One day she started to have seizures which recurred several times during the following week. When she was finally taken to a hospital, it was too late. The doctor said that the infection had gotten into her brain. She died of meningitis.

During the collective family grieving, my father wiped his tears and said: "This is the first death in our family! You should take it to heart!"

I didn't quite know what he meant by that. I was an eighteen-year-old pre-med student, bewildered by what was going on in her brain and felt guilty that I could not save her. Mang's ailment and my mother's mental breakdown created in me a personal interest in brain diseases.

A few years later, working as an intern in Taiwan University Hospital, I became familiar with meningitis. This was the time when tuberculosis was prevalent. In the pediatric ward, they had isolation rooms where about a dozen comatose children with tuberculous meningitis were lying in bed, their mothers sitting helplessly by their sides. We had to inject Streptomycin into their tiny spinal canals because the drug could not cross the blood-brain-barrier. While taking care of those children, I was suffering with them, and the anguish of the parents was more than I could bear. Whenever a child died, I cried with the family. Once, the mother of the dead child had to stop crying and comfort me: "Doctor, you have done your best!"

During the years when my children were growing up in the U.S., I was tormented by the fear that they might contract some incurable diseases, particularly the ones that I was most familiar with. Tuberculous meningitis was always on my mind because their father had TB while he was young. I would be on the lookout for warning signs: fever, headache, vomiting, neck stiffness, disturbance in consciousness or difficult in walking. I consider myself an extremely lucky parent that all my children grew up normal and healthy. Ironically, my oldest daughter, Pamela, contracted TB from a patient while she was a medical resident. This patient, whose lungs were ravaged by tuberculosis, was wrongly diagnosed as having terminal lung cancer and no precautions were taken. Pam was treated promptly, rested for a year and was cured.

Chapter 11

KUNG FU, GRASSHOPPER AND RAMÓN Y CAJAL

One day in 1971, I met a colleague, a fine neurologist, in the hospital elevator. I asked him how was he doing. He sighed and said, "I don't know what I am doing."

"What do you mean?" I asked.

"Spending my whole life trying to differentiate one incurable disease from another! We have no idea what's going on in there and don't know how to treat them."

I was not totally surprised by what he had said. I had also felt the frustration of not being able to fully understand the brain diseases. Most of them were labeled "idiopathic," meaning cause unknown. That's when I began to think twice about doing brain research.

Several years earlier, while working under Dr. Edith Potter, I had made some new discoveries on the development of human pancreas. Dr. Potter helped me write a paper and had it published in a prestigious pathology journal. The paper had received a great deal of attention, and had been frequently cited. The thrill of that discovery had made me think that I could make a contribution in brain research as well. But again, there was no one around who could teach me. Like a kid in a candy store, I was tempted by too many interesting subjects, and didn't know where to begin. The chief of the department assigned me a research project, but I could not get passionate about it.

After a year of fumbling, I found my calling in a most unusual way.

I was sharing an office with three residents. One of them was Jorge, a bright young man from Argentina. One day Jorge came over to my desk, put down a two-volume book and said: "I came across this book in the library today. I have read the original Spanish text when I was in medical school. This is the new English translation that just came out. I thought you might like to read it." There was pride on his face.

The book was written by the Spanish anatomist Ramón y Cajal, who was awarded the Nobel Prize in 1905. The book was published in 1914 under the sponsorship of the Argentine scientific community, and translated into English in 1928, the year before I was born. Lately I had been snowed under piles of newly published books and periodicals. "Do I have time to read an old classic?" I asked myself as I leafed through the pages.

Suddenly, I was struck by a photograph of the master himself sitting in front of a microscope. He had eagle eyes, a hawkish nose, receding white hair, white beard, and a slight frown on his thin face. The sharp image of the old man set against a dark background had the austere air of a Velazquez painting. His microscope looked exactly the same as the one that belonged to my grandfather. As if hypnotized I sat down and started to read. I could not put the book down.

Cajal is known as the greatest neuroanatomist in history. His voluminous work on embryonic development and the structure of the brain has laid the groundwork for modern neuroscience. In order to visualize nerve fibers which are transparent, he used a silver impregnation method that stained the nerve fibers black. The stain was a modified version of the original silver stain invented by Golgi, an Italian anatomist. The two men shared the Nobel Prize, but they were archrivals.

The only tool Cajal used was a primitive monocular microscope. His discoveries were confirmed by subsequent generations of scientists who used tools that were tens of thousands of times more powerful. His strength was his razor sharp eyes, his vivid imagination and his logical mind. After winning the Nobel prize, he directed his attention to a new field: experimental research on nerve regeneration, or the regrowth of severed nerves (Ref 1).

Cajal's experiments were conducted mainly on rats and rabbits. He observed that the peripheral nerves in the body and limbs had potent regenerating potential, but the central nervous system—brain and spinal cord—was not capable of regeneration. When the sciatic nerve in the leg of a rat was cut, the nerve ends would shrink due to its intrinsic elasticity, leaving a gap between the two ends. The proximal end that was still connected to the spinal cord would grow across the gap and within a week or two, reconnect with the distal end. Cajal had tried to prevent the regeneration by displacing the distal end or by placing obstacles in the gap, but the proximal nerve end could feel its way around, make detours and eventually find the distal end. These findings prompted Cajal to put forward a hypothesis that the distal end in the injured nerve produced a chemical substance that he called "neurotropic factor" which could attract and guide the course of the regenerating nerve. But the nature of the neurotropic factor was elusive as methods for chemical analysis were not yet in existence, and Cajal's theory remained a matter of conjecture. Years later, a famous neuroscientist at University of Chicago, who was a candidate for the Nobel Prize, produced convincing experimental evidence that repudiated Cajal's theory. After that, Cajal's theory fell to the way side.

When I finished reading Cajal's book, I became his most dedicated follower. I could see a wide open path leading from the neurotropic factor and branching out in multiple directions and infinite possibilities. I imagined that the neurotropic factor might be used in the treatment of brain or spinal cord injuries. In addition, this hypothetical factor, or the lack of it, might have something to do with degenerative neurological diseases.

Besides Cajal's brilliant scientific work, I was fascinated by his other attributes. He was a consummate artist and a gifted writer. His book was illustrated with more than three hundred pen and ink drawings, done by his own hand. These exquisite drawings looked more lively than conventional photographs. His narrative was animated and exuberant, and conveyed the secret wonders of the "realms of the infinitely small." The language was poetic and floral in the Spanish tradition. In the article "The Miracles of Histology," he wrote:

> "—the tireless lashing of the spermatozoon as it hastens breathlessly towards the ovum, the loadstone of its affections; the nerve cell, the highest caste of organic elements, with its giant arms stretched out, like the tentacles of an octopus, to the provinces on the frontiers of the external world, to watch for the constant ambushes of physico-chemical forces—"

In his autobiography (Ref 3), Cajal portrayed himself as a rebellious, unruly and adventurous young man whose first love was art. Cajal's father, a surgeon, tried to discipline him and to cure him of his artistic obsessions by sending him to be an apprentice, first to a barber and later to a shoemaker. Cajal, in his youth, was prone to depression and at one time, contemplated suicide. Eventually, he did go to medical school, where he developed a fascination with dissection. He and his father worked side by side to sketch the anatomical structures of the body which they then compiled into an atlas. In the end, Cajal gained the respect and approval of his father. The art world's loss was science's gain.

Before encountering Cajal's work, I was lost in a jungle of scientific information. Suddenly, there was Cajal, a trailblazer larger than life. He showed me clarity, direction and infinite possibilities. I felt I was in the grip of something immensely exciting, and I decided to follow in his footsteps. But first, I had to see for myself what had led Cajal to his hypothesis. So I bought ten white rats and repeated Cajal's experiment.

I began by setting up an operating table. After putting on a surgical gown and gloves, I anesthetized a rat with ether, then shaved and sterilized the skin over one leg. I made a long incision, found the sciatic nerve, a thin white thread buried within the muscle, and cut it. Then I closed the skin wound with silk sutures. On various postoperative days, I took the nerves out, again under anesthesia, prepared the slides and observed with a microscope the sequential changes that had occurred during regeneration.

But it was not as easy as it sounded. My first rat died from an overdose of ether after I took too long finding the nerve. The second rat died from blood loss, after I accidentally cut an artery. However, after dozens of procedures, I was able to complete the operation in a matter of minutes with the loss of only a few drops of blood. I could do it with my eyes closed.

One day as I was performing the now familiar procedure, a strange feeling of deja vu came over me. Had I done this in a previous life? It took me a while to recall a similar experiment I did when I was a child.

* * *

The summer I turned nine, I was conscious of wanting to be someone other than just myself. I wanted to be a kung fu master.

Kung fu master is an inadequate Western term for *wu xia* (martial arts hero), a class of people skilled in *wu shu* (martial arts) whose aim in life is to defend justice and right the wrongs in the world. They help the poor and the oppressed, and punish the wicked rich and corrupt officials. A *wu xia*'s life is the embodiment of adventure, justice, romance and mystery.

Like many boys of my generation, my sisters Lan, Na and I were obsessed with *wu shu*. My parents had never intervened, they allowed us to do anything the boys did. This attitude of gender equality was what distinguished my family from the others. As a result, my sisters and I were bold and daring, a different breed of creatures from our shy and demure girlfriends. We even had the idea that girls were superior because my brothers were younger and weaker than us girls. As soon as I was able to read, I devoured every *wu xia* book I could get my hands on. These books, some illustrated with cartoons, were as fascinating to generations of Chinese children as science fiction is to children of today.

The *wu xia* appeared at night dressed in black tight outfits, with black kerchiefs covering their faces. They sneaked into people's houses and heavily guarded mansions; they could jump straight from the ground to the rooftop or scale high walls; they hung upside down with their feet hooked to the eaves and punched holes in the paper window shade to peek into the rooms. They would leave a note of warning written in blood or cut off someone's head without ever being noticed. To be able to perform these deeds, they had to spend an entire life time practicing *wu shu*.

There were a great many *wu shu* schools, each practicing a unique style. The two famous schools, *Shaolin* and *Wudang*, were run by monks who lived in monasteries in the high E'mei mountains in Hubei province and of Wudang in Jiangsu province. The *wu shu* they had perfected, was kept as a clan secret and handed down through generations of insiders.

The *wu shu* novels abound with stories of young men who ran away from home in search of masters. They went through unbelievable hardships to reach the snowy mountain top and prostrate themselves before the masters. If they had the *yuan* (a predestined relationship or affinity) with a master,

GRANDFATHER'S MICROSCOPE

they would be accepted and put through years of grueling training. They learn to jump, to box, and to use weapons such as swords, spears, sticks and chains. The novelists painted vivid and thrilling accounts of the *Wu Shu* practice, the monks' way of life, and their heroic deeds.

The *wu xia* were almost all men, but there were a few exceptional women who somehow managed to escape the traditional feminine roles. My idol was a young woman portrayed in a novel "The Dagger Woman." Her family owned what's known as "the dagger bureau" (an equivalent of Wells Fargo in the old American west) and she was taught by her own father, the old master. Obviously she did not have bound feet. But the disappointment came at the end when both she and her sister married the same young scholar whom she had rescued from death.

The most engaging *wu xia* novels can run in a series of more than a hundred volumes. During summer breaks, Lan and I would lie in bed reading 2-3 volumes each day, not caring about food or Mother's scolding. She wanted us to read serious books and practice calligraphy, but we let her words passed over our ears like wind, and instead we would go outside to practice *wu shu*.

The only weapons we had were toy wooden swords bought from the street venders. The swords had fancy handles, decorative carvings and little mirror inlays on the shields. We tied the swords with ropes around our waists, ran around and terrorized the neighborhood boys. But we had no idea what else to do.

One day as our clan congregated in the big athletic field in front of our house, I hit upon a plan. "We have to go to Shaolin temple to find our masters," I declared. The image of myself dancing with the sword in front of the master surged into my head. The master would be a wiry, energetic old man with rosy cheeks, long white beard, bushy white eyebrows that shaded a pair of penetrating eyes. His snowy white hair would be piled into a bun on top of his head, and he would be dressed in an ancient grey cotton outfit with tight leg binders. He would jump into the air as light as a swallow, and his movements would be as swift as lightening.

"But we don't know how to get there, we are too young to find our way." Lan, ten years old, was more practical.

"We will go as soon as we are old enough to find our way." I insisted.

"But when we are old enough, we have to get married," said Na who was eight.

"We shall never get married." Lan somehow had the idea that marriage was a dirty word.

"We can get married first and when our husbands die, we can go find our masters." Na came up with this compromise.

"But the masters don't want old women." I snapped and the conversation ended there, the issue unresolved.

In the meantime, we trained ourselves in our own front yard. We practiced cogwheel turning; we ran through the veranda, then jumped across a four-foot-wide walkway and landed on a raised flower bed; we did high jumping over a bamboo laundry stick stretched over the top of two chairs. Aside from scrapes and bruises on our knees, we weren't getting anywhere close to becoming *wu xia*.

Some kid, I don't remember who, told us about the way *wu xia* trained in high jumping. They would stand in a shallow hole and practice jumping out of it with knees locked. With time, the hole would be made deeper. By the time a person was able to jump out of a foot-deep hole with knees locked and sandbags tied to his legs, he would then be able to jump freely from the ground to the roof top.

We dug a shallow hole in the big field and began practicing. But with knees locked, I couldn't even get my feet off the ground. It was very frustrating. After a while we gave up and looked around for something else to do. We found it easier to climb trees, and from a position on the top branch, we could survey what was happening on the streets below. But a smiling policeman came and told us to get down.

GRANDFATHER'S MICROSCOPE

I was walking in the big field, head bent, dejected by my physical ineptness when I noticed tiny creatures that could soar high into the air with amazing lightness and grace. They were the grasshoppers that made their home in the grassy field. They came in all sizes, shapes and colors; some were green and delicate looking, others were coarse and brown. I ran after one, and when it had landed in the grass, quickly cupped my hand over it. I missed it the first few times but with a little practice I could easily catch it.

I was puzzled by the tiny creature I held in my hand. How did it get the power to pop off like an exploding fire cracker? When I held it close, I saw that it had disproportionately large eyes and a pair of long and thick legs. There must be something hidden in those legs that enabled them to jump like that, I thought to myself. I yanked one leg off expecting to see something, but nothing came out. I then set the grasshopper on the ground. It could still jump although not quite as high as before. When I took both legs off, the grasshopper flapped its wings and flew into the air for a short distance before dropping to the ground. But with both wings and legs gone, the creature rolled pathetically into a ball on the ground, totally helpless. I did this a few times, the result was always the same, then I stopped. But I didn't tell anyone, not even Lan, about what I had done with the grasshoppers.

I was not proud of what I did, but I felt I had to do it in order to satisfy my curiosity. Little did I know that the grasshopper experiment would be the forerunner of the rat experiment three decades later when I became a neuropathologist.

At the flea market, they sold praying mantises housed in small cages made of wooden sticks. These creatures looked like green grasshoppers but they were much larger and had sharp knifelike claws and a huge mouth. I asked my mother to buy one and hung the cage from a post in the courtyard. I watched it feasting on the grass and vegetable leaves which I held through the cage bars. I wanted to see if it could jump and fly like grasshoppers, but I was afraid of its powerful claws.

One day, I went to the big field, caught a grasshopper, took off its legs and wings and presented it to the caged pet. The praying mantis quickly grabbed the grasshopper with both claws, put the prey's head into its mouth and started crunching away. Within seconds, the grasshopper was gone.

Passing through the courtyard, Lin Ma caught me red-handed. She frowned and said: "Bad karma! Killing is sinful. It is a life and has feelings like humans!"

Her remark shocked me. It had never occurred to me that grasshoppers could have feelings like us. But Lin Ma was, to me, a guru who had uncanny ways of knowing how the world works. Imagining myself a grasshopper, legs and wings torn, and being gobbled up by the praying mantis sent terror down my spine and filled me with guilt and fear. It was one of my sins that I did not want to be reminded of. In the years to come, I would also bear the burden of guilt toward the rats I had killed in the name of science.

Half a century later when I was working in Taiwan, I had witnessed a practice, imported from Japan, that was intended to pacify this guilt feeling. On a certain day, the medical school would hold a memorial service for the animals sacrificed for the advancement of science. The researchers would congregate in the auditorium, displaying baskets of flowers and candles for a massive funeral. The chiefs of the departments would light incense and bow three times in front of an imaginary casket to wish the animals successful reincarnation into the world.

Having completed my first set of experiment, I was more convinced than ever of the validity of Cajal's theory. The next step was to prove it with modern chemical methods. The last time I dealt with chemistry was in college in China some thirty years ago, and it was my least favorite subject. Now I pursued it with passion. In 1979, after years of hard work and in collaboration with a colleague who was a chemist, I was finally able to confirm Cajal's postulation. I had identified the nature and the source of the neurotropic factor in the nerve, but that was a long story (Ref 3).

*References:

(1) Santiago Ramón y Cajal (1928): Degeneration and Regeneration of the Nervous System. Hafner, New York (Reprinted 1968))
(2) Santiago Ramón y Cajal (1937): Recollections of my life. Translated by E. Horne Craigie and Juan Cano, and published by The MIT Press, Cambridge, Massachusetts,1989.
(3) H. Mei Liu (1981) Biology and Pathology of Nerve Growth. Academic Press. New York.

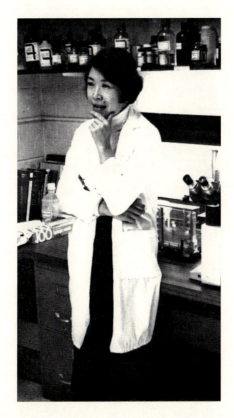

Photograph taken in Mei's lab in Providence, Rhode Island during a very productive year in her research career. 1980.

Chapter 12

FENG SHUI

My friend Naomi took me to see Turandot at the Lyric Opera in Chicago. It was the very first time I had been to a Western opera. I was mesmerized by the lovely music and the lavish production set in the imperial court in ancient China, but I thought the story was absurdly unreal. The idea that a stranger could confess his love and win the heart of a princess in imperial China was outrageous; most likely he would have been put to death just for looking her in the eye. But when Liu, the slave girl, stabbed herself to protect the anonymity of her master, I wept openly.

Naomi said to me during intermission: "You need to see a therapist!"

That was in the year 1970, and things were not going well. I was forty years old, and recently divorced after being with the same man for 22 years. I had been fired from my job as an assistant professor in a medical school. I was shocked, angry and terribly confused. It was the very first time that I had failed at things I cared about so deeply, and the messages from the outside world were in conflict with the way I viewed myself. Besides, my financial situation was precarious. I had three children to raise and I was financially responsible for my aging parents who lived in Communist China.

I said to Naomi: "Of course I am depressed and worried about the future. But I have gone through worse times than this before, and I think I can manage this one." But deep inside, I felt as if I were navigating the rapids in a lonely raft with three children and two elderly parents aboard. There was no one who could reach out to me and give me a hand. I was worried about my new habit of popping a little white amphetamine pill every morning just so I could have enough strength to get out of bed. Maybe I was in denial, putting on a brave face while deep inside I was snapping. So I made an appointment with the therapist who had helped Naomi to get through her divorce. On the second visit, I was sitting across the desk from the doctor and telling him about a dream I had had the night before.

I am looking for my mother in a crowded auditorium. It looks like a medical convention in the U.S. I reach the front row where my mother is supposed to be sitting. There is an empty seat flanked on both sides by two dark-haired women. As I approach, they turn towards me. I see that they are mixed Chinese and Caucasian, not pure Chinese, not my mother. I point at the empty seat and ask: "Was Dr. Liu sitting here?" "She just left," they tell me.

I run outside the main entrance and see a shiny, black horse-drawn carriage parked on the circular driveway. A middle-aged Chinese woman is sitting alone in the open carriage. She looks like my mother, heavy set, short hair and wrapped in fur. I climb onto the carriage and sit next to her. I stare hard at her face and talk rapidly in a language I do not understand, trying to convince her that I am her long lost daughter. But she turns her face away, not convinced by what I say. With a wave of her hand, the carriage pulls away. The sound of the horse hooves reverberates in the air.

I am left standing on the curb, my body shrinking to child size, feeling lonely and frightened.

I suppose my dream was telling me what I should have already known; that the roots of my mental anguish reach back into my childhood. But none of this was evident to me at the time. After five sessions, I stopped going to the therapist. I could spare neither the money nor the time for self-reflection.

Eventually, I did land a new job, as an assistant professor in a medical school across town. The annual salary was a paltry $12,000. It was especially low pay for a medical doctor, but rather than going into private practice, I preferred the learning opportunities and intellectual challenges of being in an academic institution.

I moved my family of four to an old town house on the near north side of Chicago, an area known as the "gold coast." The house was built at the turn of the century and sat on a narrow plot at the end of a side street near Lake Michigan. It was conveniently located. Everything was within walking distance: the hospital where I worked, my children's school, Lincoln Park, the beach, and plenty of shops and ethnic eating places. Friday afternoons, on my way home from work, I stopped at a wine and cheese shop where the manager, a white-haired gentleman, introduced me to European and domestic wines and taught me the basics of grapes and vineyards. On warm days with the front window of my house open, I could sometimes hear beautiful music floating in from the house across the street, whose owner was the principal harpist for the Chicago Symphony Orchestra. I bought season tickets to the Symphony and the Opera and went with my women friends. Slowly, my wounds were beginning to heal.

Friends who lived in the neighborhood warned me that some mysterious dark force had been looming over the houses on my side of the street. My house, the worst hit, had changed hands three times during the past five years. Each time, there was a divorce or death and the house had to be sold in a hurry before any improvements could be completed.

I suspected that the house, perhaps the entire neighborhood, was suffering from bad *feng shui*. *Feng shui*, meaning wind and water, is based on the ancient Chinese belief that man is the product of nature, and his house and burial place must be so constructed as to be in harmony with natural forces. The style and location of any man-made construction influence the *qi*, the breath or energy, which flows in the universe, circulates through human bodies, and affects human life and destiny. *Feng shui* demands that a person's door be facing a certain direction, that his bed not lie beneath a beam, that a bowl of goldfish be placed strategically in his living quarters. A person who lives in a house with bad *feng shui* would be plagued with bad luck. And if a person is buried in a grave with bad *feng shui*, the bad luck would pass on to that person's offspring. That's why people would consult *feng shui men* before buying or building a house, burying the dead, getting married, opening a new business and other auspicious occasions.

I wasn't an expert, but the house did not look like it carried much good luck with it. The red sandstone exterior was crumbling, and the interior was in a shamble.

But bad *feng shui* or not, I had snatched up the house at an affordable price. I jokingly told the neighbors: "It's a good thing I am already divorced. Maybe my luck will change and I'll get married!"

My realtor, a kind, middle-aged Jewish lady told me with a secretive smile that an Italian count once lived in that house. It almost sounded like the setting of a gothic novel, except the house was not a mansion, it was just middle class.

The reputedly haunted house (center) Mei lived in on the near north side of Chicago. 1975. Photograph by Mei.

Family photography. From left to right: Mei, Deborah, Peter and Pamela. 1975.

I hired workers to repair the cracked ceilings, to strip the old wallpaper and paint the walls off-white. After putting down my oriental carpets, piano, Chinese chest, rosewood dinning set and hanging my Chinese scrolls on the walls, the house became a lovely and comfortable home for my family of three children and three cats. I kept a lookout for signs of a ghost, but there were none.

One day I chanced upon the realtor in the supermarket. The woman greeted me warmly and congratulated me for having broken the record. In her memory, no one had lived in that house for three years. The realtor admitted for the first time that the house was haunted.

"How do you know it's haunted? Have you seen the ghost?" I was teasing.

"Yes, in fact I did see him."

"Him? When?" my curiosity was piqued.

"Remember the day I took you to see the house? I was waiting downstairs in the living room while Cindy took you upstairs." Yes, I remembered Cindy, owner of the house, she was blond and attractive.

"I was sitting on the sofa looking out the window when, out of the corner of my eye, I saw a shadow passing. I turned around as he materialized at the top of the staircase." She paused to take a deep breath.

"What did he look like?" I was swept up by the tale.

"I only had a back view of his lower body. He had knee breeches and high boots, definitely a thing of the past." Her enormous eyes were glistening.

"Has anyone else seen him?" I persisted.

"Not that I know of." She was gloating over her ghost-seeing eyes. "Several people who lived in that house were driven to distraction by strange noises like metal clinking in the middle of the night. It sometimes shook the whole house."

When I first moved into the house, I had also heard the loud clinking noises, but had attributed them to a faulty heating system. The furnace in the basement had been converted from an old coal-burning boiler. When the furnace was automatically ignited, there was a loud boom like an explosion, and the gas flame would shoot through the cracks of the large coal-loading door. I hired a contractor to replace the antiquated furnace and to let out the air bubbles trapped in the pipes and registers. The noise had since stopped.

My next door neighbor Virgie, a lovely and intelligent woman of Austro-Hungarian ancestry, had become a good friend. She was a few years older than I, born and raised in Chicago, and lived by herself. She treated me like a sister and my children like nieces and nephew. I asked Virgie if she knew anything about the Italian count.

"He was a tailor from Sicily." There was a forbidding tone in her voice.

"What happened to him, do you know?"

"He was gunned down in front of the house. The assassin was hiding in the portico leading to the basement. It was during the time of the gangland killings. Corpses were left in the doorways and along the streets. It was awful."

So this Italian ghost had been seeking a substitute and driving people mad! Lucky for me I had more or less pulled myself together by the time I moved into this house. My *qi* was strong enough to resist the ghost.

It was certainly not my first experience living in a haunted house. My previous home on the south side of Chicago was cursed as well. As soon as we moved in to the charming old house with its large bright rooms and white marble floors, everything started to go wrong. The old furnace exploded, shaking the house and wrecking the chimney; fortunately no one was hurt. My marriage faltered and finally failed. Things soured at work and I eventually lost my job.

After the divorce, I sold the house to a dashing, well-to-do young black couple. The husband's mother, a thin, elderly woman with an authoritative manner, paid for the house in cash. During the closing, the wife leaned over and whispered to me: "I refuse to be maneuvered by her." It was a remark I thought odd. When I was briefing the new owners about the neighborhood, the husband was visibly upset upon hearing that a black alderman was living next door. A few days later, I stopped by the house to retrieve something I had left in the garage. The house was swarming with militant-looking young black men who made me feel uneasy. Before long I read in the newspaper that the new owner was charged with hiding a female fugitive with whom he was allegedly having an affair. One day the young wife poked a gun into her Afro and pulled the trigger. She had killed herself in the same master bedroom where I had once sunk so deep into despair that suicide seemed to be an option.

My children were still young and more or less oblivious to the tragedies unfolding in the house, but I later learned that my son Peter experienced the ghosts as well.

"Yeah, I had a poltergeist hopping around in my bathroom when we lived on the south side," Peter said with a sweet smile as if he was talking about his pet. "He was a mischievous little guy, not hurting anyone, just making noises." Peter was about ten at the time. Now at age fourteen, his poltergeist had evolved into a full-fledged ghost. He told me, in no uncertain terms, that his grandmother's ghost had come all the way from China to live with us.

"The ghost already in the house would not let her in," Peter said in all seriousness. "She has to fight him."

"Did she win?" I asked dubiously.

"Yap!" Peter replied firmly. He had welcomed his grandmother into our house.

I remembered an old Chinese saying about young boys. Their strong *yang qi* enables them to see things that adults could not see. In my loneliness and despair, I hoped that Peter was right and that my mother's ghost had come to live with us.

While I struggled to keep my head above water, to survive at my new job and to properly raise my three children, I was also worried constantly about my family back in China. During the 1960s and 70s, the country was thrown into a series of man-made disasters. The first was the great famine of the early 1960s, brought about by the delusional miscalculations of Chairman Mao Zedong. At first, the government was in denial, and the famine was kept a secret. But as millions died from starvation, the government finally gave in and allowed overseas Chinese to send money and food packages to their needy relatives.

Fortunately, I had a loyal friend, Kong Shu-mu, who was a businessman in Hong Kong. Each month, he purchased, on my behalf, money orders and as many relief packages as permitted by law and sent them to my parents. These two-pound packages contained flour, rice, lard, sugar, or powdered milk. My father would divide the food into smaller packages and distribute them among my relatives. These relief packages were more precious than money; there was no food for sale even on the black market.

As the famine began to lift, Mao Zedong, fearing criticism and revolt both from within his party and from the general population, staged a nationwide campaign of terror, called the Cultural Revolution. His goal was to eliminate those who did not agree with his policies. His victims included high government officials, professors and intellectuals who dared to disagree, even the "Old Marshals" who had fought and won the civil war were not immune; all were branded as "bourgeois counter-revolutionary elements." They were humiliated, tortured, and sent to prison or to labor camps in remote areas. Countless people committed suicide. Students, incited by their political leaders, organized themselves into a youth army group called the "Red Guard." They were for the most part lawless thugs who wandered the country terrorizing people and destroying property. The Cultural

Revolution lasted more than a decade (from 1966 to 1976) and had a long-lasting, devastating effect on the psyche of the Chinese people.

At the time, the U.S. was allied with the Nationalist government on Taiwan and was therefore considered an enemy of the People's Republic. Any Chinese person with ties to the U.S. was in danger of being persecuted. My letters and packages home were always funneled through Hong Kong, but I was in constant fear that people would find out where I really lived.

My family did not dare tell me in letters what was happening, I could only imagine their suffering and despair. I also did not tell them what was going on in my life. I didn't actually lie to them, but I simply stopped referring to my husband in my letters. It took me years to muster the courage to tell them that I had been divorced. By that time, they had already guessed what had happened. I suppose my parents were disappointed, for they believed that couples should stay together for the sake of their children, as they had. They were worried that I might not be able to properly raise my children all by myself. But they were wrong.

When my children were growing up, they considered themselves regular all-American kids. We spoke only English at home. I had made half-hearted efforts to teach them my mother tongue, but afraid that they might grow up with a Chinese accent, I abandoned those language lessons at the first sign of resistance. They wanted to be the same as everyone else. I didn't force them to be different.

As an immigrant, I was also keen to assimilate into American society. We always lived in mainstream middle-class neighborhoods where we were inevitably one of the few minority families. When we went to Chinatown for dim sum, I always felt out of place. The sights, sounds and smells were familiar, but the shop owners spoke neither Mandarin nor English. Since I did not speak Cantonese, I felt like a foreigner.

My children said they were glad they didn't have to grow up in such an untidy and noisy place.

It took me many years to realize that we might have been better off if we had belonged to one of those communities. They were often like a big village, a home away from home. People from the same village in Guangdong province brought their relatives and neighbors to Chinatowns and re-established their clans. Within each closely-knit community, there were always older people who would baby-sit, talk stories, play chess, sing songs and run errands for one another. Reading books by Maxine Hong Kingston and Amy Tan, I realized that these drab places had been the roots, shelter and inspiration for countless American-born Chinese, and had provided a sense of community that we never had.

Decades later when I heard then-First Lady Hilary Clinton proclaim that "it takes a village to raise a child," I realized the extent of deprivation my children had suffered. They did not have a village or relatives; they had only a mother who was struggling to keep body and soul together in a foreign land. All of my worries had worn me out. I was constantly irritable and non-communicative. But they were good children; they hid their feelings and never complained. They knew their mother loved them above everything in the world although they did not understand me and they feared me sometimes.

I didn't realize at the time that I was growing up with my children. Newly single and trying to "find myself," I was going through the adolescence that I never had. There was never enough time to do the things I wanted to do: to explore new places, new cultures, to learn about the arts, music, literature, and architecture. I felt like a person who had just been released from a long prison sentence and wanted to make up for lost time.

It would be false to say that I was not interested in romance. I looked everywhere for someone with whom I could share interests, and a sense of comfort, trust and respect. I desperately longed for a tender and lasting relationship and had fantasies about marrying again.

As soon as I began to take a man seriously, catastrophes would happen. Once I had planned a rendezvous with a lover in Europe. We had arrived separately but somehow could not find each other in the strange city. Walking with another lover on a rocky promenade along a seashore, a dense fog appeared from nowhere. Our vision was totally blocked and we were afraid to take a step. Another time I gave a dinner party at my house and introduced a suitor to my close friends. During the party my favorite Siamese cat disappeared without a trace.

Whenever a man got close to me, an alarm bell would ring somewhere deep in my head. I would have nightmares about a giant snake with cold slimy skin crawling under my bed cover, and I would experience the horror of the dragon boat ghost all over again. I would hear my mother's voice: "He is not trustworthy!" "He'll hurt you!" "He is possessive and will make you a slave!" "If you don't dump him, he'll dump you sooner or later!" I would often pronounce a man guilty until proven otherwise. I would not give anyone the benefit of a doubt. Why should I?

I had seen the image of my mother's disastrous marriage reappear over and over again. I knew so many men and women whose lives had been ruined by failed marriages. I had also heard horror stories about conflicts between children and their stepfathers. I swore I would never let that happen to me and my family.

I remained a cynic. It was only in my old age that I came to realize that my conception of love and marriage had been terribly distorted by my mother's dragon boat ghost. There were plenty of good marriages in this world, but I never seemed to notice them. My eyes only saw what they were programmed to see: the pain, the misery, the boredom and the despair of failed marriages.

In the end, I took the easy way out, and, like my father before me, I blamed my own failures on fate. I decided that I was destined to lead a lonely life, and that neither marriage nor money was in the cards.

But in giving up on the idea of finding a mate, I started developing a feeling that something else was about to happen, and it had nothing to do with men. I was vaguely aware of a new agenda that was being laid out before me, although I could not clearly see its design. It was my task to find out what was required of me, and no one was about to distract me.

The realtor lady was a little too premature in congratulating me for having survived in the haunted house. A few months later, I was on the move again.

I had problems getting along with my boss. My application for promotion to associate professor was denied, despite having published many research papers and co-authored a book entitled "Brain Tumors in the Young." The atmosphere was very tense, and I decided to leave. Before long I was offered a position as an associate professor at the newly established medical school of Brown University in Providence, Rhode Island.

My two youngest children were reluctant to leave their school, their friends, and the familiar places that had long been home. I too was sad to say goodbye to the city. Pamela had to stay in Chicago though; she was starting medical school in the fall. I was beginning to wonder how I would pay the medical school tuition which amounted to my entire annual salary.

An unexpected help came, this time from the ghost in the house. I could not believe my good luck when my realtor told me that she had sold the house for twice the purchase price. I put the proceeds in the bank and told Pamela: "Here is the money for medical school. I told you not to worry. Someone up there will provide."

I did, however, give myself a small reward: a lithograph by Picasso.

Chapter 13

THE YALE DREAM

When I walked into the hospital morgue on a fine summer morning in 1988, the world appeared to be in excellent order. The room was spotlessly clean and permeated with the odor of sweet cider from paraformaldehyde, a disinfectant. A man's body was lying on the table, and at his feet, stainless steel instruments had been neatly laid out on a tray.

Generally speaking, autopsies were done by residents, but we were short of residents those days. Consequently, I had to do the jobs of four persons: resident, attending physician, teacher, and medical researcher. But it was not as intimating as it sounded. With the help of a capable morgue attendant, Bill Stewart, we got the autopsies done fast and clean. We had worked together for three years, and we made a good working team.

In the locker room, I changed into a scrub suit overlaid with a green surgical gown. I put on my surgical gloves and walked to the right side of the corpse while Bill went to the opposite side. I said to him: "O.K, let's go!"

The case was a robust man in his fifties who was DOA.

The medical examiner had authorized the hospital to perform the autopsy and to give him a copy of the postmortem report. The man looked like a blue-collar worker judging by his large muscles, calluses on his hands and by his facial features.

I put a new blade on the scalpel, and made the Y-shaped incision. Then I switched to a six-inch long knife and used it to cut the skin and muscle away from the bones of the sternum and ribs. But the knife was dull as it had been during the three previous autopsies. Several times I had asked Bill to sharpen the knife, but he just ignored it. Feeling a little irritated I said to Bill across the table: "Bill, the knife is very dull, have you sharpened it lately?" No response.

"Look, I just can't cut. Could you sharpen it now?" I asked again.

"Go sharpen it yourself!" he roared.

I was startled by his remark. His eyes were wide and his face flushed. He looked threatening, but I was not about to set a precedent.

"But that's your job!" I protested.

"You are always bossing me around! Who the hell you think you are? You bitch!" He shouted at me; he had never done that before.

I was shocked. People in my professional and social circle never used that kind of language. I felt my anger rising and my brain searched the bad name file. Without thinking I blurted out the words: "You wife-beater!"

That word sent him into a rage. He picked up a sharp-pointed long knife from the tray and started brandishing it in front of my face and yelling in a hoarse guttural voice.

I didn't hear a word he was saying, I was stricken with terror. My own words reminded me of what he was capable of doing.

Bill had a long history of domestic violence during each of his four short marriages. Now this crazed, burly, forty-year-old, woman-hater was waving a butcher knife at me! He was standing between me and the steel double door which was shut. If I screamed, nobody in the corridor could hear me. The scenario was not pretty.

I heard a soft whisper coming from behind my left shoulder: "Take a deep breath! Don't panic! Don't make a sound or a sudden move! Don't look at him! Keep on working!"

Some mysterious mechanism took over, gears shifted inside my head. The fear suddenly dissipated into the air, and I felt nothing, no emotion or any kind. Without a word, I resumed the dissection. I had my eyes fixed on the work in front of me but I was watching Bill out of the corner of my eyes.

Five or ten minutes passed, Bill was still ranting and raving, but the anticipated racial slander did not come, it meant he was not totally out of control. I slowly put down my knife and walked to the telephone on the wall to my right. With my back facing Bill, I took off my glove and dialed a number. When it was answered, I said in a low voice: "Dr. Friedman, you had better come to the morgue right away, it's urgent."

Entering the room a minute later, J.D. Friedman, esteemed director of anatomical pathology, immediately turned pale.

"Bill! .... eh, Bill! Why don't you put that knife down and come to my office, we can talk," J.D. stammered. After several minutes, Bill grudgingly obliged, and I was left alone to do my work.

I found the cause of death, a blood clot, only a quarter of an inch long, that had blocked the major coronary artery in the heart. Then I proceeded to finish Bill's job: sewing up the body, cleaning the table, washing the instruments and putting them in a pan of disinfectant. After tidying up the morgue, I went to my office to write up the postmortem report.

Thank goodness it was a Friday. At the end of this traumatic day, I got into my car and headed towards Cape Cod. As my car climbed over the Sagamore Bridge, I looked down at the shimmering blue water in the Cape Cod Canal, and I felt like a bird in the sky. I drove to Woods Hole and stopped at Duck Soup, a quaint little restaurant, and had a plate of fried oysters. At 8 pm, I went to the Marine Biology Laboratory to hear a lecture by a Nobel laureate. Then I drove twenty-five miles to my hideout on the Cape.

The streets were dark and deserted. The night air was permeated with scents of newly cut grass and summer flowers. When I unlocked the squeaky door to my cabin, I felt a strange mixture of peace and elation. As I opened the windows to let in the fresh sea air, I heard crickets singing in the grass. At night, I was lured to a dreamless sleep by the sound of a foghorn as I tried to let the image of the madman with the knife wash away.

I woke up at dawn by the chirping of birds outside my window. I got out of bed, put on my running shoes and headed for the beach. A few blocks of deserted streets later, a breathtaking vista spread before me. The soft rays of the early morning sun were descending on the marshland that separated the town from the ocean. The marsh was covered with tall golden grass and had a long narrow wooden bridge stretched over its top. The bridge was slightly sinuous and had the look of rustic handmade furniture. I walked along the edge of the marsh and followed a meandering stream where the water was so clear you could see the pebbles on the bottom. Clusters of mussels were clinging to the mud on the river bank.

At the end of the stream was a little pond that was home to hundreds of birds and seagulls. They were resting on the water or circulating slowly in the air. Periodically, a bird would drop like a stone into the water, diving with wings tightly held to its sides.

GRANDFATHER'S MICROSCOPE

I sat cross-legged on the bank of the pond, eyes closed, breathing deeply the moist salty air and trying to erase memories of civilization from my mind. I imagined myself a seagull living on this pond that had everything I needed: family, companion, fresh air, delicious meals, no traffic jams, no striving for success, no jealousy, no hostility, no money worries and no stress. For a moment, I was bathing in tranquility and bliss, at one with nature. As I got up to leave, the birds turned to watch me. They must be wondering, "Why is it leaving? What's the hurry?"

I bought the cabin during the summer Deborah finished her sophomore year at Wesleyan University. We were driving through Cape Cod on our way to vacation on Martha's Vineyard when we chanced upon this jewel of a town tucked away on the north shore of the island. The town of Sandwich sits next to the Cape Cod Canal that separates the Cape from the mainland of Massachusetts. The town center had picturesque colonial houses, duck ponds, small white churches with pointed steeples, a glass museum and a historical museum containing pictures and relics left from the whaling days. The place seemed to have taken a step back in time; it's the oasis that I had craved.

A few years earlier, I had published my first book "Biology and Pathology of Nerve Growth." While fulfilling my hospital obligations during the day, my writings had to be done at nights, and on weekends and holidays. When the book was finally in print, I was at the point of physical and mental exhaustion. But the book failed to gain recognition by the neuroscience community. Also, I was not able to get a grant to continue my research.

Shortly after the publication of my book, I had two unexpected visitors from China. They were old classmates back in medical school in Qingdao. The husband, Dr. Zhou Huiming was the head of pathology and his wife, Dr. Shi Zhenrong was the head of ophthalmology in our Alma mater.

They were highly respected authorities in their fields. My friends were quite impressed with my book and had persuaded me to let them take it back to China and translate it into Chinese.

During the preceding three decades, the Chinese government had banned English. Now with the Chinese door opened to the West, the medical and science communities were trying to make up for lost time. But the younger generation had not yet learned English, so they had to depend on Chinese translations. My friends were among the few who had learned English before the Communist liberation. So they had committed themselves to translating important medical textbooks from English to Chinese.

A year after my friends had returned to China, I received by mail, the Chinese translation of my book. It was a small paperback with a blue cover. The paper and the photographs were of poor quality. The letters were simplified Chinese characters (adopted by the Communists) that were totally foreign to me.

"Who would read something like this?" I put the book away and forgot about it.

At the time, I was exhausted and disenchanted with research; I thought I needed a change. Much to my surprise, I received an offer to be an assistant dean at the medical school. Although I had some reservations, I felt I couldn't afford to turn it down. The world would laugh at me for my lack of courage, and the men who had competed for the position would be thrilled. "Who knows? I might be good at this!" I told myself, and I accepted the offer despite warnings from friends.

I quickly found out that administration was not my cup of tea, it was more difficult than scientific research. In research, I was my own boss and I called the shots. In administration, I was an insignificant part of an establishment that was tainted with power struggles and prejudices. During the year of my tenure, I had managed to make some powerful enemies who had conspired to make it impossible for me to do my job. My application for promotion to full professorship was unjustifiably denied. I was humiliated and defeated. On top of it all, I had chosen to resign from the local Neurological Society in protest of their policy of holding the monthly dinner meeting at a private club that excluded women from membership. After that, I became totally isolated, increasingly angry, and the world responded with either indifference or hostility. It had become a vicious cycle. Nothing in my life had worked the way I wanted.

I was confused not only about the world around me, but about myself. When I was twenty years old, all I wanted was to be a doctor and to take care of my family. But now I had so much more needs, compulsions, and a burning desire to achieve some seemingly unattainable goals. Maybe I was to blame for my own misery. What had happened to that timid girl whom everyone liked? Why had I changed so much?

Once again, my *qi* had become so low that I became physically ill. Now that the nest was empty, the foods I prepared just piled up in the refrigerator. To lose my normally hearty appetite was a sign of serious trouble.

The sight of Sandwich and its environs had restored my zest for life. I fell in love at once with the place. Lucky for me the housing market in the New England area was depressed. I bought a little wooden cabin that had no foundation and no heat, but it had a toilet, and a propane stove for cooking. In a way, the cabin reminded me of the little hut I lived in while I was a refugee in Taiwan.

The cabin had turned out to be my salvation, an escape into the world of sanity. When I returned from my morning walk on the beach, I would turn on the radio and tune to WGBH in Boston. I cooked my favorite sea foods, attended to my little flower garden, and read correspondence, news magazines and novels.

In my hand was a letter from my niece, Tong, who was living in New Haven. Her husband was an assistant professor of physics at Yale University. In her letter, Tong had enclosed a copy of an article published in a Chinese overseas magazine. The article was written by my talented elder sister Lan, Tong's mother. It was in Tong's voice, and I translate it here.

* * *

Grandfather's Yale Dream

No one in our family drinks alcoholic beverages, and we seldom have drinks around the house. But at parties, I like to sidle close to people with drinks in their hands. A whiff of the aroma of liquor would instantly bring me back to my childhood and to the memory of my grandfather.

My grandparents had been living in our house before I was born. I remember the evenings when the house was illuminated by the soft lemon glow of a lamp and permeated by delicious cooking fumes. Grandmother would call from the kitchen, "we are having something good tonight!" That was a prompt for Grandfather to get out his custom-designed carafe, a square glass bottle with lead filigree. He would send my uncle to the wine shop down the street to buy four ounces of burning wine (rice liquor). He had no use for beer or grape wine claiming they were tasteless like water.

Grandfather was not given to lengthy conversations, but a glass of burning wine could unlock the talking box inside him. What he talked about were not some earthshaking tales of mystery, they were events he had experienced in the past. Grandfather had an amazing memory and could recount vividly events that happened long ago down to the last detail: dates, places, names of the persons involved. No matter how many times we had heard them, they never lost their freshness. Grandfather often got so carried away by his own tales that he forgot to eat the spicy, taste dishes Grandmother brought before him.

What had made the deepest impression on my childhood memory was the story about his medical school experience.

Grandfather was born to a scholarly family at the end of the Qing dynasty. At age six, he was sent away to his uncle's house to be taught by a private tutor. Grandfather was slow and stubborn, a trait for which he was punished with daily beatings. His skin was regularly covered with wounds and scabs to the point that he could not take baths in the summer. At age nine, he contracted dysentery and almost died. When he recovered from the illness, a miraculous change took place; he became smart and attentive and was at the top of his class ever since.

While attending a boarding school in the city, he received devastating news from his hometown. His mother, about forty years old, was stricken ill with severe abdominal pains. All the traditional doctors in town were sent for and all kinds of herbal medicines, secret potions and ashes from the temples were tried. Prayers and promises to the gods were offered, but to no avail. His mother's early death was a terrible blow and made Grandfather realize the importance of modern medicine. He vowed that he would one day become a good doctor and help his people. After graduating from high school, Grandfather entered the foreign medical school, Hsiang Ya, founded in 1914 by American missionaries. He was the only student in his hometown to have passed the difficult entrance examination. One can imagine the stir it created among his folks, the men with pigtails and women with small bound feet.

When in 1916 Grandfather began his freshman year at the Hsiang Ya medical school, he was full of confidence and optimism. The easy-going and fun-loving country lad was soon dazzled by the sights and sounds of the provincial capital of Changsha. He had underestimated the difficulties ahead of him. Grandfather was fluent in the Chinese classics and his mastery of the English language was good enough. However, the high school he attended in the country did not prepare him adequately in basic sciences. Also, seeing foreigners with blue eyes and yellow hair for the first time was indeed intimidating. Grandfather recalled the experience years later.

"Those American teachers! They talked as though they had hot turnips in their mouths. I couldn't understand anything they said except for 'waterrrr'!"

At the end of his freshman year, Grandfather failed chemistry and biology. He was dismissed and his dream collapsed.

Later in life, even though he had made a good living, his failure in medical school was the regret of his entire life. Many times he told this nightmare to his children, and later to his grandchildren when he was a white-haired old man.

"I had a dream about Hsiang Ya again last night! I had this exam paper in my hand but couldn't understand one word of it! What an anxious moment! What terror! I was covered with sweat when I woke up!"

"Was that Hsiang Ya medical school really that hard?" I couldn't believe a smart man like my grandfather could fail in anything.

"And how! The Hsiang Ya medical school was something no ordinary person could manage! Forty of us started out, and we were eliminated one by one. By graduation, only a few were left. Those few were geniuses!" He had endless admiration for those Hsiang Ya graduates.

"What would have happened if you had managed to stay on and graduate?" I was curious about the alternatives.

"That would be unthinkable! Those Hsiang Ya graduates are now authorities in medicine, red-hot national figures. If I were among them, I wouldn't have to buy my own liquor." Grandfather laughed and stroked his beard as he indulged in this fantasy.

Grandfather did not achieve distinction in his career. He worked hard to feed and educate his ten children, a formidable task in times of war. He had hoped that at least one of his children could fulfill his dream of becoming a doctor.

The person who had succeeded in fulfilling Grandfather's dream was my second aunt Mei. While a medical student, Aunt Mei and her fiancee went to Taiwan. After graduating from medical school in Taiwan, she went to America to practice medicine. During the next thirty years, circumstances had prevented Aunt from coming home. The letters and money she sent home could not relieve Grandfather's longing for his favorite daughter, especially during the years when my grandmother was stricken with a strange illness.

"If only your Second Aunt were here! She is an American doctor, she can cure your grandmother's illness." Grandfather thought the world of American medicine.

The Chinese doctors had no idea what was wrong with Grandmother. She started out with clumsiness of fingers and could not button her clothes. Her hands became weak; she could not hold the rice bowl. Then she couldn't walk. For the last four years, she was confined to bed having lost the use of her limbs as well as bladder and bowel control. Her mind began to fail. "Where am I? My bed was not here before!" She kept on asking these strange questions: "The window used to be there, not here." "What's going on? Why am I sleeping in a bath tub and not in my bed?"

They had tried everything from modern medicine to traditional herbs and acupuncture, nothing helped.

After Grandmother's death, Grandfather lost his appetite and stopped drinking. He said everything tasted bad, he ate just to stay alive. He often called me to his room and let me sit opposite him while he lay on a rattan recliner. He would tell me those stories. Besides the familiar Hsiang Ya dream, he had a new dream:

"I had a wonderful dream last night! My appetite was back again! I was sitting at the dining table enjoying a scrumptious banquet! When I woke up, I still had the delicious taste in my mouth!" I realized he was always dreaming of things he had lost. He died at age 83 of a heart attack.

Because of Grandfather, I had a great respect for the medical profession although I am not doctor material. I have inherited from my mother a love for the arts. My mother was a frustrated artist, and she had paved the way for me to enter the art world. After graduating from an art institute in China, Aunt had helped me to come to the U.S. for further studies. I am now a graduate student at the famous Yale University.

While studying art design, the course director gave the class an assignment: to use a "time line" to illustrate the important activities of an institution. During my research for my assignment in the Yale library, I found an interesting book entitled:"Yale in China" (Reuben, Holden), published in 1964 by the Yale-in-China Association Inc.

From this book, I learned that the Yale-in-China Association was founded in 1901 by young men of the Yale Christian Association. The major emphases of the mission were: "education, the improvement of public health, the introduction of Western culture and more importantly the Yale spirit—a spirit of sportsmanship and fair play, a sense of honor, responsibility, honesty and manliness."

Earlier attempts to evangelize Hunan were among the most heroic in the history of missionary work due to anti-foreign sentiments growing out of a spirit of nationalism. The missionaries were repeatedly refused entry into the cities or driven out after a few months of residence.

Some had to live on a houseboat anchored in the river outside of the city wall, they made daily visits to the city selling books and preaching Christianity. But the missionary workers considered the hardship a special challenge since "the blood of the martyrs is the seeds of the church." Some of these young men had indeed become martyrs. Thornton, who became the first official head of the Yale-in-China mission, died of tuberculosis in 1904, and Seabury died of accidental drowning in 1907.

In 1906, they had established a medical branch in the form of a dispensary with only one physician, Edward H. Hume. A school of nursing was established under the direction of Nina D. Gage. Dr. Hume was soon joined by Dr. F.C. Yen who had a M.D. degree from Yale University, a doctorate in Tropical Medicine in England and had worked in the African Congo.

The medical branch grew rapidly in popularity and demand. In 1911, in accordance with a petition made by eighty leading citizens, the Hunan government and Yale Mission made an agreement "The Hsiang Ya Agreement" (Hsiang is short for Hunan, Ya is short for Yale) to build a complete medical school and hospital. The government would provide the site and money for building the medical school, a nursing school and a dormitory, and pay the general expenses of running the school. The Yale mission agreed to build a hospital from private donations, to provide all medical equipment and to recruit and pay the salaries of American medical graduates who were willing to come and teach. Dr. Yen became the first president of the Hsiang Ya medical school and Dr. Hume was the first president of the Hsiang Ya hospital.

After reading the book, I have come to appreciate the remarkable contributions and the sacrifices of the early American missionaries. It was the first time I understood the meaning of the word Hsiang Ya, Yale in Hunan.

> The book showed several photographs of Hsiang Ya faculties and students during the early years. I searched for Grandfather among the young men wearing traditional long gowns and watermelon hats. One man with glasses looked somewhat familiar, but I could not be sure if it was Grandfather.
>
> It's miraculous how things had come full circle and how the lives of three generations in our family had been changed by Yale-in-China. Imagine if Grandfather had not studied in Hsiang Ya, Second Aunt probably would not have studied medicine. If Aunt had not studied medicine, she would not have come to the States and neither would I. If I had not come here, I would not have found Grandfather's Yale Dream.

No one would have imagined that seven decades later and across half of the globe, I had became Grandfather's alumnus.

As I read my sister's article, I could not stop the flood of tears. I was filled with profound feelings of loss, regret and homesickness. I had one comforting thought though. No matter how disappointing my career had seemed to be, no matter what a failure I thought of myself, I was, in my relatives' eyes, a success.

Chapter 14

THE EAST WIND

One spring evening in 1988, the telephone rang. I thought it was someone from the hospital, instead the vaguely familiar voice of a Chinese man was on the other end. It turned out to be an old friend named Yang who had left China on the same boat I did four decades ago.

"Have you heard the news about CC. Guo?" Yang asked me.

"No, what about him?" I drew a sharp breath and my heart skipped a beat.

"He is in the hospital, terminal cancer."

The news shocked me and filled me with grief, but also brought back fond memories of our past.

I had first met Guo the day we went out digging graves in the barren hills of Qingdao. It was during our second year of medical school. Our anatomy professor, Dr. Shen, was particularly interested in bones. We had to spend countless hours memorizing their Latin names, and drawing pictures of their anatomical minutia and of the tiny holes the nerves and blood vessels pass through. In the beginning, the class only had one set of bones, not enough to go around. The young assistant professor told us to go get our own bones from unclaimed graves in the countryside.

The night before, I discussed the grave-digging expedition with my parents. My father was appalled. Robbing graves was a great sin, one that would offend the spirits of the dead and bring down their wrath. After much discussion, Father finally consented, but instructed me to burn some incense, and say a prayer of apology to the ghost afterwards.

Our little group of two women and four men started out early on a chilly autumn day. The sky was overcast and grey. We set off on a narrow dirt road leading into the nearby countryside. The terrain grew hilly and more remote. Finally, we came to a deserted plot with unmarked burial mounds scattered throughout. Three of the young men congregated around one mound and began to dig while the girls watched.

It was quiet all around. There were no birds chirping, no human voices, only the clanking of the hoes hitting the gravel. The grave was shallow; soon a rotten wooden coffin came into view. The men jumped into the pit. They started hacking at the lid of the coffin, pulling back the wooden fragments. Inside, they found a skeleton covered with fragments of black silk cloth and long strands of dried dark hair. It was an eerie sight on this chilly, barren hillside.

Suddenly, I heard a strange noise coming from behind me: a low, hoarse moan followed by a suffocating sound. The sound, so creepy and sinister, sent a cold shiver down my spine, and my hair stood on end. I froze for a moment and then slowly turned to peek over my shoulder.

It was not a ghost, but Guo sitting on the ground, his back hunched and face buried in his hands, sobbing uncontrollably. To that point, no one else had shown any outward sign of weakness. We had come mentally prepared for an unpleasant task. Given the fact that Guo was a gregarious, tough guy and an ex-soldier, his distress was quite unexpected. We were all stunned and didn't know what to say.

When Guo had calmed down, the men put the bones into a burlap sack and took turns carrying it back to school. We soaked the bones for several days in strong acid. After a thorough scrubbing, they turned out white and clean.

Later, I learned that the sight of those bones in the unclaimed grave had reminded Guo of his younger brother, who was a soldier in the Nationalist army. During a recent military campaign against the Red Army, the brother's division was decimated. All the men were presumed dead or captured; the whereabouts of Guo's brother was unknown. Not long after the episode at the grave, Guo changed his major from medicine to biology. Within a year, the mainland fell, and Guo was among the last load of refugees to arrive in Taiwan.

A year later, Guo's brother suddenly turned up in Taiwan. He had been captured by the Communists, but had managed to escape. I didn't know the details of the story, but there must have been a lot of weeping when the brothers were reunited.

Guo was a robust man of immense vitality and integrity. He spoke our native Shandong dialect and swore like a soldier. He walked "with a tiger-like stride that make the wind whistle." But underneath the rough exterior was a man of gentle spirit, true intelligence, and a delicate artistic temperament. He was a problem-solver to whom everyone turned for help. During our years of exile on Taiwan, he was the pillar of our little group, a big brother for his friends and uncle for his friends' children. He would literally take the shirt off his back and food from his mouth to give to others.

During the year Guo did his graduate study in the U.S., he came to stay for a short while in our house. He was quite taken with Pam, my oldest daughter, and claimed her to be his goddaughter (he had three sons). For decades, we maintained our friendship through an annual exchange of Christmas cards and family photographs. Then Guo, a professor and leader in his field, began urging me to bring my children to Taiwan for a six-month sabbatical.

"It's time you should come back and see old friends! You would not recognize the place, there has been such progress. You could make a big contribution here on Taiwan. There is not a single neuropathologist on the whole island!" Guo had written.

I had enthusiastically agreed to his suggestion, but as a stream of friends and relatives began arriving from China, I had to postpone my visit year after year. Then, in a Christmas card, Guo wrote: "If you don't come this year, you will never see me again!" It sounded like a jest; but I had a sense of misgiving. In his last photograph, Guo did not look well. He had lost a lot of weight, and his eyes were listless. Five months later, my good friend was dying from pancreatic cancer.

That night, Guo came to me in a dream.

We are walking on a dirt road in the country. Guo is ahead of me, carrying something like a hoe on his shoulder and he looks the same as he did when he was a medical student. We arrive at a thicket at the foot of a hill. He goes to a grave mound, and starts digging and shoveling dirt away. We jump into the grave, and it turns into a cave that has stone walls. There is a narrow passage that leads to an opening where light is filtering through. We file into the passage which is barely wide enough for one person. As I approach the opening, the earth shakes, and the cave begins to collapse. I look back to see Kuo lying on the ground. His abdomen is crushed under a huge rock. He motions for me to go forward as if this is a very important mission.

The following morning, I booked a flight to Taiwan. By the time I arrived at Guo's bedside, he could no longer speak, but his mind was clear. He wanted me to tell him about my recent trip to China. As I showed him the pictures I had taken of our alma mater and of our class reunion, his large eyes were full of longing. For years, he had wanted to go visit his old home and old schoolmates, but, at the time, the Nationalist government on Taiwan had forbidden government employees (including teachers) to visit Communist China.

The following week, I visited Guo every morning at National Taiwan University Hospital. Each time I passed through the cavernous front hall and walked down the long corridors, I was gripped with sad, tender remembrances. This was the place where I attended classes and did my clerkship nearly four decades earlier. Next to the hospital stood the New Park where my lover and I took our evening walks among the pagodas and over the little bridges arching across the lily ponds. Beyond the New Park was Hengyang Street, which was once the downtown district of Taipei. The old-fashioned bookstores and silk shops were still standing, but the glamour had passed on to other newly-developed commercial districts.

At the invitation of an old schoolmate, who was a prominent professor of marine biology, I gave a lecture at National Taiwan University. After lunch, we took a stroll down memory lane. Forty years ago, this friend had also taken refuge in one of the little tool sheds at the athletic field where I once made my home. The athletic field was still there, but the tool sheds were long gone. The little stream that used to run along the field was now covered over by high-rise commercial buildings. The university still looked the same, but its surroundings had transformed from a sleepy agricultural land into a bustling metropolis. As I glanced around, it was disorienting. I felt as if I were in a dream.

That week, I was also invited to the opening ceremony of the newly established biomedical division of Academia Sinica, the equivalent of the National Institutes of Health in the U.S. The president of the division was my classmate from medical school. The laboratories were filled with new, cutting-edge equipment, far better than what was used at most American medical research institutions. The administration was trying to recruit Chinese-American scientists to return and work at the institute.

I was immediately impressed by what Taiwan had to offer. But there were other surprises as well. I found I no longer had a language problem; everyone spoke fluent Mandarin. In the years since I had sailed away, the population, it seemed, had fully embraced mainstream Chinese culture.

Two weeks after I got back to Providence, news came that Guo had died.

Since that trip, I had not been able to concentrate on my work. Seeing my dying classmate had greatly moved me, and had made me realize how much of my life had already passed by. But I was also intrigued by what I saw of Taiwan, and by how the place where I once sought refuge had grown and changed. So much progress had been made, but there was still a need to fill those gleaming new laboratories with experts who could teach the next generation of scientists. I felt that there might be something that I could contribute. So I signed up for a six month sabbatical (the only one during my twenty years of academic career) and prepared to take a position with Academia Sinica.

In Taiwan, I was surprised to learn that my expertise in neuropathology was in great demand. I was immediately invited to give courses and lectures in medical schools and hospitals throughout the island. I was happy that I finally had a chance to pay back the debt I owed from four decades earlier—to the Nationalist government for giving me food, shelter and a medical education, and to the Taiwanese people for their friendship.

During my stay in Taiwan, I was warmly received by my former schoolmates who treated me as if I were a long-lost relative. It was a feeling I had not so far experienced. At the end of my sabbatical, I ended up extending my leave of absence. Finally I resigned from Brown University and accepted an invitation to be chairperson of pathology at the newly established medical school of Cheng Kung University in Tainan, on the southern end of the island. In addition to teaching and practicing pathology, I had to oversee the daily workings of the clinical laboratories for the 700-bed hospital. In this demanding new role, my neuroscience research was put on the back burner.

One day, I came across a notice in a neuroscience journal about the 4th International Congress on Neural Regeneration which was to be held in Pacific Grove, California. It was fifteen years earlier, at the 1st Congress in Las Vegas, that I made a presentation of what I thought was an important new discovery. I had found that a major population of cells in the nerve, called Schwann cells, were capable of producing a nerve growth factor (NGF) after nerve injury. I had produced evidence using modern biochemical tools that the NGF in Schwann cells was the same NGF originally discovered by Rita Levi-Montalcini in 1964, in mouse salivary gland. Furthermore, I had predicted that the NGF produced by Schwann cell was the equivalent of the "neurotropic factor" postulated by Cajal nearly a century earlier.

Slide review session with the staff in the Pathology conference room, Cheng Kung University Medical College, Tainan, Taiwan. 1990.

When I submitted my paper to the prestigious journal, Experimental Neurology, it was reviewed by Dr. William Windle, founding editor of the journal, former chief of neuroanatomy at NIH and a pioneer in neural regeneration research. In his critique, Dr. Windle wrote: "This paper is very important and should be published without delay."

But the rest of the neuroscience community considered my findings outrageous; they had held on to the dogma that only mouse salivary gland could produce NGF. To my knowledge, no one could explain why only sexually mature, male mouse produce a potent NGF in its salivary glands, while female mouse and other animal species do not. But it seemed so logical to me that Schwann cells should produce NGF following nerve injury. I imagined that Cajal would be intrigued by my findings.

At the 1st Congress, my paper received a very cold reception and my findings were dismissed outright. I was so humiliated that I could not bring myself to attend any of the subsequent Congresses. But after a decade, I finally felt ready to return, not as a participant but as an observer, and learn about the latest discoveries. After the meeting, I planned to go to LA to visit my daughter Pamela and her husband Ken. She was an assistant professor in internal medicine at the University of Southern California Medical School.

During the pre-conference reception at Pacific Grove, a man approached me. He was in his mid-forties, and looked vaguely familiar.

"Have we met before?" I asked.

"Yes, we met a long time ago, during the 1st Congress," he replied.

It occurred to me that this man was a postdoctoral fellow at the time; he had asked me some questions about my research.

"Imagine," he laughed, "they didn't believe that Schwann cells make NGF!"

I was stunned. I thought to myself: "Do they believe it now?" But I did not want to appear ignorant, so I didn't pursue the matter.

As it turned out, in the years that I had been away from the U.S., scientists had made great progress in the technique of genetic analysis. They had found the DNA of NGF in Schwann cells, indicating that Schwann cells produce NGF. My findings had been confirmed, but no one bothered to credit my work. Only a few people who had attended the 1st congress even remembered it. Nevertheless, I was overjoyed by this new discovery; it meant that I was not delusional and I was on the right track. Once again, my confidence was restored.

One day, during lunch at the convention dining hall, I spotted a young Asian woman sitting alone at a table. I took my tray and sat next to her. She turned out to be a graduate student from Shanghai. It was the first time I had met a neuroscientist from mainland China. I hesitated for a moment before asking this question: "Have you ever read a book called 'Biology and Pathology of Nerve Growth?"

"Of course I have read it! Every one has read it!" the young woman exclaimed. "That book was the reason why I became interested in neuroscience!" It took me a while to gather the wind to say: "I am the author of that book." She looked incredulous.

As soon as I returned to Taiwan, I felt like I had been given a new lease on my research life. I obtained a generous grant from the National Science Foundation in Taiwan and resumed my research. By this time, nerve regeneration had become a major focus of investigation. Scientists were attracted to the field by new and exciting discoveries in basic sciences. Rita Levi-Montalcini who had discovered NGF some 20 years earlier, was finally awarded the Nobel Prize.

For the following three years, I taught a team of young neurosurgeons to do neuroscience research. We were able to extend the scope of my work on NGF in Schwann cells, and to develop new methods for aiding nerve regeneration. We had also come up with some new insights into the mechanisms of stroke in the brain. When I was asked by an international journal to write a review article on the state of the art of nerve regeneration, I felt that the time and effort I had spent on neuroscience research was not in vain.

I suppose that once I had returned to Taiwan, it was inevitable that I should find my way back to mainland China. During the meeting in Pacific Grove, I had become acquainted with Dr. Yu, a young neuroscience professor at Stanford University who had been organizing meetings that brought together American scientists and their counterparts in China. At Dr. Yu's invitation, I went to Beijing to be a speaker at the International Congress of Neuroscience.

In Beijing, I had the chance to meet a number of leading Chinese scientists. After the conference, I and other conventioneers went on a tour of the Great Wall and other famous historical sites of this ancient city. I found everything I had read about Beijing to be true, and like my father before me, I was captivated by the scenery, the history, the culture and the warmth of the people. For me, a trip to Beijing would have been incomplete without a visit to the Peking opera and a taste of the Peking duck and the Mongolian lamb that my father had praised.

It was on that trip that I finally made it back to my "old home."

After the meeting in Beijing, I flew south to Changsha, the city of my birth. I had arranged this visit through the Yale-in-China Association in New Haven. During the flight to Changsha, fragments of my childhood came flashing back like a broken motion picture. It was surreal to finally arrive at the hometown I did not remember, but had dreamed of my entire life.

If my father could see the Hsiang Ya Medical College now, he would be dazzled by the great changes. The small clinic established nearly a century ago had grown to a massive institution with three affiliated hospitals in Changsha and many more throughout the province. Nearly everyone in the healthcare profession in the province was a graduate of either the medical school or the nursing school.

At the time of its inception, Hsiang Ya Medical College was considered one of the two leading medical institutions in China. The other one was Union Medical College in Beijing, founded by the Rockefeller Foundation. There was an old saying: "Union in the north and Hsiang Ya in the south." During the war with Japan, Hsiang Ya Medical College had to relocate; the faculty and students fled first to Guiyang and then to Chongqing. After the war, the school, renamed Hunan Medical College, was faced with the difficult task of rebuilding itself out of near total ruin. After 1978, when the Chinese opened their doors to the West, Hunan Medical College was able to resume a relationship with the Yale-in-China Association. Each year, the association recruited college graduates from the U.S. to teach English to the medical students and faculty. So far, no American doctors had come to teach at Hsiang Ya.

Across the street from Hunan Medical College was the Hsiang Ya Hospital, which had retained its former name. Both the medical school and the hospital had dormitory compounds that housed several thousand employees and their families. In the evening, the street in front of the hospital that led to the Hsiang River, was bustling with shoppers, and ablaze with lights from gift shops, fruit stands and fast food vendors. The paths were crowded with employees returning home on foot or on bicycles. They were yelling in a Hunan dialect I had not heard in ages. The air was thick with the pungent, peppery aroma of Hunan cooking, which was unlike anything else in the world. Fresh red hot peppers sauteed in boiling lard with fermented black beans, green onions, ginger and garlic released fumes so potent that my eyes and nose smarted. Strange that a cooking smell should have such an emotional impact on me. As I sneezed, tears flowed down my cheeks and I was overcome with nostalgia.

For the umpteenth time, I said to myself: "How I wish my parents were here!" I remembered a poem that I learned as a child:

> I left home young and not till old do I come back
> My accent is unchanged, my hair no longer black
> The children don't know me, whom I meet on the way
> Where'd you come from, reverend sir? They smile and say
>
> By: He Zhizhang
> Translated by Xu Yuan-Zhong in
> "Three Hundred Tang Poems, A New Translation."
> The Commercial Press, Hong Kong. 1996

The sights, sounds and smells of the place of my birth opened the door to long buried memories and powerful longings. Here, I came face to face with my father's Hsiang Ya Dream. I felt deeply drawn to this place that he so revered, and I realized that if I came back to work here, I would truly be living out my father's dream.

One rainy morning as I looked out from the second-floor window of my room at the guesthouse, I saw a quaint old brick building. It was the old dormitory of the American missionaries and one of the few original buildings still standing. I thought of the American doctors who had voluntarily left their comfortable world to embrace a life of misery and sacrifice in a strange and inhospitable land. They had suffered immense hardship, but ultimately they had triumphed in the name of Christ. Although I am not religious in the conventional sense, I was taught the same values: humanity, honor, courage and a belief in the goodness within oneself. I saw my parents' faces and heard their collective voices: "You have been blessed with good fortune, it's time you shared your blessings with others."

In 1995, I returned to Changsha and became a professor of neurobiology. For the following three years, I taught neurobiology and neuropathology to a new generation of Chinese students and young faculty members. I also established a scholarship fund in the name of my father, and the annual interest of the fund went to selected medical students from poor families.

The faculty members and students there treated me like a long lost relative, for I was the first American-trained professor who had returned home to teach. The person who was responsible for my personal welfare was Dr. Yang Dongliang, director of foreign affairs, who was also a professor of pharmacology. Dr. Yang made arrangements for me to visit the famous places in the region, and he personally accompanied me to visit my old hometown.

Chapter 15

THE WOMEN WARRIORS

The last time I saw Thin Aunt was around 1935. I was a six-year-old girl and she a pretty, demure teenager. We called her Thin Aunt not so much because she was slender (which she was), but because the word "thin" means "small" in Hunan dialect, and she was the youngest girl in my mother's family.

Close to six decades later, I took a four-hour train ride from Changsha (long sand) to Hengyang (eternal sun) to pay Thin Aunt a visit. The teenager of my memories had become a white-haired, eighty-year-old lady living in a plush apartment with her daughter and son-in-law, both of whom were schoolteachers. Thin Aunt still had the same look I remembered: a quiet poise, a twinkle in her eyes and a determined mouth. For three days, her family treated me to feasts of rare delicacies that took days to prepare.

And almost without a pause, my aunt "talked stories" to me about our family's past.

My aunt said to me: "I have to tell you something that impressed me most about you," she remembered with a smile. "I was with your mother in the hospital when you bounced into the world with such speed and vigor we were caught unprepared. There you lay, naked, screaming with all your might. It was late in the eleventh moon, the coldest time of the year. A drop of water turned into ice before it hit the ground. But the plum tree outside the window was showing lovely pink blossoms. That is where your name, Hsiang Mei, Hunan's plum blossom, came from. Plum is the national flower of China, it symbolizes hardiness, thriving in the face of cold and adversity." Aunt paused for a moment while she recalled something else.

"Your mother was very impressed with the Hsiang Ya Hospital, the first of its kind in Hunan. Everything in the hospital was clean, white and shining. Many of the doctors and nurses were Americans. That was the first time I saw foreigners. At first, I was so scared I did not dare to look straight at them. They looked fearsome with pale faces, huge eyes and yellow hair, but they were gentle and kind, always smiling." Thin Aunt talked as though it were yesterday.

"There were some Chinese girls who were learning to become nurses. Your mother said to me, I am envious of these nurses. They have an admirable profession, and they are independent. That's when I decided to become a nurse, and it was a lucky decision."

My aunt recalled another story: "When I was growing up, I seldom saw my father. Nai Nai was old-fashioned and didn't pay much attention to the children. So I looked up to my big sister, your mother. Big Sister was intelligent and capable, she took charge of the household while my father was living abroad. My father treated Big Sister like a firstborn son because he believed in the equality of men and women. This kind of attitude was very unusual at that time."

"One morning I heard a knocking at the front door, and a man's voice called out: 'Palanquin ready for the Big Miss'. Big Sister, only sixteen, came out of her room and went to the front door. She stepped into the palanquin and sat down. The coolies were ready to hoist the carrying poles onto their shoulders when she saw the maid and me peeking out from inside the gate. 'Want to come for a ride, little sister?' I nodded, climbed in and sat beside her. We rode through the streets, passed the old city gate and came to the countryside where there were farmhouses and fields. The palanquin stopped at an open field where a lot of peasants were gathering. Two young men who looked like students from my father's school came forward to help us out of the palanquin. Big Sister followed the young men to the front of the crowd of men and women in tattered clothes. People stared hard at this big-footed young woman dressed in a crisp white muslin top and long black skirt."

"Big Sister started to speak: 'Uncles and Aunts, times have changed. We are living in a new world now. In the old world, there were many evils. You worked hard all your life, yet you suffer hunger and misery. Why? because you can't read letters. Now we are going to wipe out the past evils. We want all children, even girls, to go to school to learn letters, so they will have a better life when they grow up.' "

"Then she turned toward the women who were huddled in one corner. 'Aunts! You all know what misery and suffering it is to be a woman and to have bound feet. That is an evil custom and it is going to stop. There is a new law that says women and men are equal. Women can do the same job as men and they can inherit money and property from their parents. So, I beg you to stop binding your daughters' feet and send them to the new school for girls in town. When your daughters gets their learning, they can have jobs, make a good living and take care of you in your old age.'"

"Big Sister's propaganda paid off. The girls' school had a steady rise in enrollment. Big Sister became assistant to the principal, Miss Ren, and helped establish the Women's Association, the first of its kind in the region. When she was in high school, Big Sister was already an aspiring writer and had published several articles in our father's newspaper. She wrote an article urging women to have self-respect and not to become men's 'play things.' To this day, that article is still in the city council archives, a historical record of the early days of the women's movement."

"In the evening when my father came home, he would talk to Big Sister about things I did not understand, like 'freedom,' and 'women's rights.' In later years, I realized they were talking about the important social changes brought on by the May 4th movement. My father had big plans for us children, he wanted each of us to pursue a profession that would be of use to the country. Big Sister was good with numbers, so she was chosen to study economics. My younger brother was to become an engineer. And my father brought a microscope from Japan for me to study medicine."

I felt a sudden jolt! I thought Grandfather had bought the microscope for one of his unborn grandchildren who would one day study medicine. But what Aunt said made more sense. The microscope was a gift from my grandfather to his youngest and brightest daughter. This new knowledge somehow made me feel guilty for having considered myself the rightful owner of that microscope all those years. I felt as if I had stolen something from my aunt.

"I never got to know my father, but I felt that his spirit was in that microscope. All my life, I have dreamt about the microscope and wished that I had it with me. After his death, all his belongings were confiscated, but somehow your mother had managed to salvage it."

I looked out of the window, and imagined my mother, as a young woman, running through the house, looking for a place to hide the microscope and the book of Shakespeare that my grandfather so valued. I was startled when I realized that my aunt was speaking to me.

"Have you ever seen the microscope?" Aunt asked me.

"Yes, I saw it once or twice, it was magnificent!" I sighed. "I too believe that it was the embodiment of my grandfather's spirit. I owed everything to that microscope. It was the reason I became who I am today! Too bad we had to leave it behind when we were escaping the civil war. It must have been trashed, no one in that backwater place would have had any idea what it was!"

It was my turn to ask a question.

"Do you remember anything about my grandfather's death?" I asked my aunt.

"In the morning, soldiers came and took him away. Shortly after lunch, my cousin came running into the house, panting and yelling to Nai Nai: 'Aunt, things have gone bad, hurry up, think of some way to save his life!' "

"Nai Nai was out of her wits, and Big Sister was away in college. Out of desperation, Nai Nai sent me to General He Long's house. She told me to kneel down before the General, knock my head on the ground and beg him to save my father's life. He Long was my father's best friend and honorary principal of the high school. But at the time, nobody could have saved my father," Thin aunt continued.

(Years later, He Long became a top military commander in the Red Army and a member of the Politburo. Unfortunately, during the Cultural Revolution, he was persecuted along with the other Old Marshals).

"After my father's death, soldiers came and ransacked the house. They took away a lot of things. Nai Nai cried all the time. Life was terrifying and we didn't know what would happen next. Big sister dropped out of college and stayed home to take care of things. The following year, she got married and the whole family moved to live with her in Changsha. Your father was like a father to me, he sent me and my brother to the best boarding schools in Wuhan, a short distance away from where you were living."

"When your family moved north, we remained in our boarding schools. Everyone thought you would be back in a few years. No one expected that within a year, the war with

Japan would break out and we would be separated for ten years."

"When the Japanese army invaded Wuhan, I decided to take my brother and join the tens of thousands of students and teachers who fled inland. I was sixteen and he was fourteen. We left with the clothes on our backs and a backpack containing a map, a quilt and two extra pairs of straw sandals. We walked on foot, climbed mountains and crossed streams. Our feet were covered with blisters; when they burst, they left the raw flesh rubbing against the straw. It felt like walking on pins and needles, the pain was excruciating. But we dared not stop, the enemy was right behind us. There was no time to think or to feel sorry for ourselves."

"Each night, before dark, we had to find a designated village or farm on our map. If we failed to find the place, we risked exposure to the elements or encounters with the wild wolves which prowled the area. The Nationalist government had ordered the local magistrates along the way to provide assistance to the students. The local people, who were themselves poor and hungry, were always cordial and would let us into their houses. People who lived in the backwoods and in the mountains were mostly illiterate and had no idea what was going on in the outside world. They were curious about why we were running and where we were going."

"The folks would boil water and spread a bundle of hay on the dirt floor for us to sleep on. After soaking our feet in hot water, we would pierce our blisters with a needle and sprinkle salt over the sores. We had to be brutal to ourselves in order to survive. Besides salt, the only medicine we had was cloves of raw garlic to cure diarrhea. Then we settled down and had our first meal of the day, a steamed wheat bun washed down with boiled water."

"We had to budget our money carefully in order to make it last till the end of the journey. That meant we were always hungry."

"Some students managed to thrive in the harsh physical conditions. Others succumbed to hunger, illnesses, exhaustion, and mental breakdowns. Some simply collapsed while walking on the road, and had to be pulled on a cart by fellow students. With no medical care and no rest, it was a march to the death."

I imagined the heart-wrenching scenes: old women with bound feet crawling on hands and knees, mothers carrying babies in their arms, bombs exploding, and families separated. All these things had happened in the cities in which we had previously lived. If our family had not moved to the north, we probably would not have survived the war.

"Someone in your family had *fu*. You were protected by the ancestors." Aunt said.

Thin Aunt and her brother survived that long march and eventually reached an area safe from the fighting. She then enrolled in a nursing school which offered free tuition, room and board. She scraped together enough money for her younger brother to go to Wuhan University to study engineering.

I had fond memories of my uncle, a cross-eyed, funny-looking youth with thick glasses. When we were kids, we looked forward to the days when he would come home for visits from boarding school. He was more like a big brother than an uncle.

During the war, my father was particularly worried about my uncle. He was the youngest and the only son of the Hsia family. The food at boarding school, my father thought, could hardly keep a growing boy alive. Despite our own hardships, my father managed to send Uncle some money through the black market, with the instruction to go out and eat some liver and spinach.

Months later, my father came home from work one day and stomped into the living room. Without a word he handed a letter to my mother. She read it and silently put the letter on the table for us to read. It was a three-page letter from

Uncle. He acknowledged receiving the money, but said he had used it to pay for something much more important: cosmetic eye surgery. He then went on to give an anatomical description of the surgical procedure: shortening of muscles in one eye, cutting a slit on the outer corner of both eyes and creating extra eyelid folds. The procedure not only would correct his strabismus, but would make his eyes larger with double eyelids. He drew pictures of his eyes before and after the surgery to show that it was worth the money.

No one said a word. I was furious with my uncle for being vain and frivolous. My family could have used the money to buy much needed food and clothing for the children. It was only much later that I understood what my lonely uncle was doing. He must have thought the only way to find a suitable mate was to improve his looks. And for some young people, a good marriage was more important than good health.

After Thin Aunt graduated from nursing school, she was assigned to work in an army hospital. That's when she met her husband, an officer in the Nationalist Army and a recent graduate of the prestigious Whampoa Military Academy whose director was Generalissimo Chiang Kai-shek. Uncle Xie was recuperating from a shrapnel wound inflicted during a battle with the Japanese. In their wedding picture, uncle Xie was an impressive looking young man in army uniform. He was tall and handsome, with large round eyes and thick uplifting eyebrows. He had the presence and persona of a General.

During the war, while Uncle Xie was fighting on the front line, Aunt and her two babies lived in Chongqing. They had a hard time living through constant air-raids and food shortages. When victory finally came, they thought they had a new lease on life. Uncle Xie was assigned a good government job in his hometown Hengyang, and their life was full of joy and promise. But their dream was quickly shattered by the raging civil war. Weeks before the mainland fell to the Communists, the Nationalist army began evacuating the family members of military officials to Taiwan. The men were to stay behind to lead the defense against the Communists. But Aunt refused to leave, she resolved that the family would stay together no matter what. They never got out.

After the Communist victory, Uncle Xie was denounced as an enemy of the people and sent to prison, where he did hard labor for ten years. After his release, he was assigned to work in a factory. Then the Cultural Revolution erupted. Several peasants he had never seen came to the city to arrest my uncle. They took him to the countryside, staged a struggle meeting and declared him a "right-wing counter-revolutionary element." He was sentenced to forced labor in the countryside, and was not freed until the death of Mao Zedong and the fall of the Gang of Four.

Uncle Xie first went to prison as a young man at the prime of his life. When he finally won his freedom, he was seventy-two years old. Only a year after his release, he died of pancreatic cancer.

"You have never seen anyone so tortured with pain and rage!" said Aunt.

I was moved to tears hearing this awful story. But Aunt simply stared at her desk, her jaw set squarely, her face impassive.

My cousin came into the study with dishes of candy, preserved plums and spiced watermelon seeds. Looking at this five-foot-six, gracious and intelligent woman, I had nothing but profound admiration for my aunt who had somehow managed to raise her five children under unimaginably cruel circumstances.

"I was lucky to have Nai Nai with me all those years." said my aunt. "While I worked as a school doctor, she cooked, cleaned and cared for my children. We were living in a typical farmhouse: three rooms, a dirt floor and a little plot of land. We planted vegetables, raised chickens for eggs and a goat for milk. Before going to school each morning, the children, from six years on, fed the livestock and watered the vegetables. After school, they fetched water from the public well in buckets on shoulder poles."

"As the only health care provider in the area, I took care of the school children and their families. Twice a week, I walked ten miles to attend political indoctrination meetings in town, then spent the next day walking back. There was no bus, no bicycle, not even a mule cart."

"Then in 1960 came the great famine, millions of people died of starvation. People ate everything: grass, tree bark, roots and even mud. Everyone had a yellow sunken face, swollen hands and feet. Children suffered the worst, they had swollen bellies and cried for food all the time."

"Nai Nai was so hungry she could not get out of bed. One day, she was on the brink of death. She said to me with her last thread of breath: 'Hurry, get a pound of pork, boil it, let me eat it and I will die in peace.' "

"So I went to the local butcher and begged for a pound of pork for my dying mother. The man was indebted to me, for I had once saved his son's life. But all he had was a pig's foot. I took it home, boiled it in water until the meat fell off the bones. I gave the meat to Nai Nai slowly, a little bit every few hours. The children didn't even get a taste. After eating the pig's foot, Nai Nai got out of bed and went on living for another twenty years. Nai Nai died in her sleep at age ninety-three."

I was amazed hearing these tales of Nai Nai. When she was living with my family, she was bored, unhappy and an opium addict. Through a sad twist of fate, Nai Nai was forced to become a hard working and responsible person. I doubt if Nai Nai was capable of being truly happy but at least she was healthier and felt needed. During her later years, she was venerated as a sage. The women in her community regularly came to her to seek advice.

"What happened to Lin Ma?" I asked my aunt.

"She became a sad and lonely old woman, a bitter fate to the very end!" Aunt told me the final chapter of Lin Ma's life story.

Lin Ma's son grew up without parents, and never learned anything good. He smoked opium and squandered away Lin Ma's hard-earned money. Finally, Lin Ma and her daughter-in-law conspired to throw the bum out of the house. People said that Lin Ma was too harsh on her son, but she had to keep him from taking food out of his child's mouth. Lin Ma' son was eventually found dead on the street one day. When the Japanese invaded, Lin Ma's grandson, barely fifteen, was forcibly taken by the Nationalist army. He was taught how to fire a gun and then sent off to the front line. He died on the first day of battle.

Thin Aunt had written to my parents about the tragedy, but they didn't have the heart to tell Lin Ma. When the war ended, my parents wanted her to stay with us for the rest of her life, but no one could dissuade Lin Ma from her dream of going home and enjoying a peaceful old age with her grandson. When my parents told her the truth about her grandson's death, she refused to believe it. My father had no choice but to find someone to take her home. When Lin Ma reached home, she found her son and grandson gone, and her daughter-in-law had gone blind and lived alone in a hut. Once again, the feisty, stoic Lin Ma accepted her fate; she took care of her blind daughter-in-law who was practically a stranger to her. When the daughter-in-law died, Lin Ma was cared for by a state-run nursing home for the elderly.

My father kept a regular correspondence with Lin Ma and periodically sent her small sums of money. In Lin Ma's letters, written by professional letter writers, she was always asking how the children were doing. I know Lin Ma would never spend the money Father sent her, but it must have been a measure of comfort to know that she had a family who cared for her. There was always the worry that in the event of Lin Ma's death, people around her might continue to collect money from us. To make sure that Lin Ma was still alive, my parents periodically drilled her on the birthdays of one or another member in the family. Lin Ma passed the test with flying colors until the very end.

One spring night, the story goes, a flood came and swept her away. She lived to be ninety-two.

When I said a tearful goodbye to my aunt, I knew it would be our last farewell. She was quite frail and had a serious heart problem. I was grateful to have had two days with her, but it was not nearly enough. I didn't have time to tell her how I came to "find" my grandfather's microscope.

One day in the early 1980s, I was driving through a small town in upstate New York on my way to visit a friend in Syracuse. I stopped for a break and casually browsed through a roadside flea market. Suddenly, I noticed a rusty brown contraption sitting amongst a pile of dishes and kitchen utensils. It was an old microscope that had the same size and general appearance as the one belonged to my grandfather. I looked it over carefully. It was made by Leitz, the oldest microscope-maker in Germany, and the year 1885 was engraved on its stand.

The owner said that he had acquired it at a yard sale, and had no idea who the original owner was. I quickly paid the asking price of $55, knowing that I would never see another one like it again. I imagined the original owner to be a teacher of biology who had lived around the turn of the century. From the signs of wear, it appeared that he or she must have gotten a lot of use, as well as joy, out of this microscope. After hours of cleaning with a copper polish, the century-old rust gave way to a golden copper tube, an almost exact replica of my Grandfather's microscope.

I took my new discovery to my laboratory, where the once mystical instrument of my childhood was dwarfed by the microscope that I was using at the time, a room-sized electron microscope. But every so often I would pop in a slide and look through that primitive copper tube, just to remind myself of the old dreams that eventually brought me here.

Chapter 16

THE MARTYR

I walked behind two men on a stretch of bumpy dirt road and came to an empty plot of land strewn with broken bricks and overgrown weeds. One of the men, officials of the municipal government, pointed to the site and said: "This is it." On one side stood a leaning octagonal pagoda with its exterior pockmarked and covered with soot; on the other side, a row of shabby houses rested against a broken wall. A corner convenience store carried the sign: "Little South Gate," the only reminder that this forbidding place was once the site of the old city wall.

From a box, I took out a stack of coarse yellow paper printed with messages for the dead and placed it on the ground. One of the men took a cigarette lighter out of his pocket, and lit the paper and the incense in my hand. Holding the incense above my head with both hands, I faced the pagoda and bowed deeply three times. As a gentle breeze blew the smoke across the empty plot, I closed my eyes and tried to imagine the scene that was played out here seventy years ago.

A young man walks down the road escorted by a band of soldiers carrying guns on their shoulders. The man is wearing a grey Mandarin robe. His hands are tied behind his back with a wide band of red cloth. The cloth crosses in front to form an "x" and is tied into a large bow on his chest. It's the "five flower big tie" traditionally used on criminals as they are led to the execution ground. The man is slightly built and thin; his walk is firm and defiant. The soldiers escort him from the courthouse in the center of town down South Street, which is flanked with low houses. A crowd gathers, people yell and run after them. They pass through the South City Gate, turn left and come to the empty plot outside the city wall. The soldiers stand the man against the wall; they line up, raise their guns and fire. The first bullets pierce the man's back and knock him down. He staggers to his feet shouting: "Freedom of speech!" A second round of bullets hit his head and silence him forever.

The event was reported in major newspapers throughout China on May 20, 1925. The man was my grandfather; he was 39 years old.

A studio photograph of the Hsia family, taken shortly before the death of Mei's grandfather. From left to right: Nai Nai, Mother, First Aunt and Grandfather. Sitting on the floor are Thin Aunt (Left) and Uncle (right). Circa 1925.

* * *

From an early age, I considered my family members peculiar, and the most mysterious of them all was my maternal grandfather, Hsia, whom I had never seen. The few times when his name was mentioned, my father would bow his head, sigh and change the subject. I couldn't tell whether the sigh was a sign of grief, respect or reproach.

What kind of person was Grandfather? What crimes had he committed to deserve death by execution? These questions periodically surfaced in my mind, but I did not dare ask my parents. The only person I was not afraid to ask was Lin Ma, who had an answer to everything from gods to ghosts. But whenever the subject of Grandfather came up, Lin Ma would bow her head and show the same kind of deference as she did to the gods. Although she had little understanding of the nature of Grandfather's greatness, she knew he was a great man because he forbade foot-binding and opium-smoking.

"Your Ma was your grandfather's favorite," Lin Ma told me. "She is understanding and capable. He treated her like his firstborn son and sent her to college in Shanghai. Your Nai Nai's favorite is your Thin Aunt, she is cute, very smart and obedient. No one liked your First Aunt, the lazy, disobedient one. Midmorning, the master would yell to her in the courtyard: 'Get out of bed this minute or I will kick you to death!'" Lin Ma's face darkened and she spit on the ground.

Another time, Lin Ma told me: "Your grandfather promised your first aunt to a boy for marriage. The boy was an engineering student and came from a good family. But the engagement had to be broken when she got into trouble."

The only physical evidence of my grandfather was an old family photograph of him, his wife and four children, taken shortly before his death. He also left behind the book of Shakespeare and the German microscope he brought back from Japan.

It wasn't until recently that the truth about my grandfather began to reveal itself to me.

One day, when I was nearly sixty years old, I received a strange letter from First Aunt in Shanghai. First Aunt, who had never written to me before, informed me that she had uncovered some important information about my late grandfather. As a result, Grandfather was soon to be honored in a forthcoming martyrs' celebration in Beijing. Aunt urged me to come and attend the ceremony. The news, coming out of the blue, sounded like a fantasy. As far as I could remember, she had never mentioned her father to me, or indicated any interest in him. After checking with my sisters in China to make sure that our aunt had not gone mad, I went to Shanghai to meet with her. I was overcome by curiosity and a sense of filial obligation.

I was waiting in the lobby of the International Hotel in Shanghai when a little old lady with a large cake box under her arm approached the information desk. There was something vaguely familiar about her. It took me a while to reconcile the image of this white-haired lady with the pretty and vivacious young woman in my memory. At age seventy five, First Aunt looked wiser than before, she seemed to exude an inner peace.

First Aunt, whose name was Yun (cloud), grew up in the shadow of her older sister and as a child was regarded as unpromising. At the time of her father's death, Yun was only fourteen years old and had no clear knowledge about her father's life. At the age of sixteen, she became pregnant with an illegitimate child. She had to drop out of high school and left her infant daughter, Lian (lotus), with a peasant family. Lian's growth was stunted, she had a squint and a hearing impairment because of an untreated ear infection. Six years later, Aunt had her second child, a boy named Yiwu. At first she kept the existence of her children a secret from her extended family. When it was eventually discovered, my mother agreed to let Aunt and her two children to come live with us.

First Aunt had no hobbies, and did not like housework or playing mahjong. She liked to wear pretty clothes and roam about town. However, as far as her children went, she was a strict disciplinarian. She spent a lot of time supervising their studies in the hopes that they would one day become someone she was not. She was hoping that her children would *zeng qi,* avenge their mother. But Lian was a slow learner because of her hearing problem. Aunt regularly vented her anger and frustration by beating the poor child whose cries and screams could be heard throughout the household.

The life of a second wife and a lady of leisure was intolerable for this intelligent and energetic woman. After the war, Aunt became increasingly restless and at the age of thirty-five, she decided to go to Shanghai to seek a career. When she left home, I sighed with relief; her departure meant that my mother finally had room to breathe.

Aunt left her four children, aged two to sixteen years, under the collective family care. A year later, her youngest child, Mang, died of meningitis. Her death aroused a great deal of collective guilt.

In Shanghai, Aunt found a job as an accountant, and for the next twenty years, she lived alone quietly, ate whatever she wanted and saved her money.

After her retirement, she kept busy by taking care of her grandchildren, who all came to Shanghai to attend school. In her spare time, she practiced calligraphy, and became quite skilled at the art.

During my years away from home, the old hatred I had felt for my aunt eventually wore out and was replaced by a genuine feeling of kinship. By the time I saw her again, my parents had both passed away, and she was my closest relative of the older generation. For three days, we sat in my hotel room in Shanghai reminiscing about my grandfather and the past we shared. This is the story First Aunt told me.

* * *

"My father was born to a wealthy family. His father, a merchant and land-owner, was uneducated and therefore belonged to the lowest rung on the social ladder. In old China, scholars and teachers were at the top, followed by officials, farmers, artisans, and merchants in that order. My grandfather decided that his two sons were to receive the education and respect denied him."

"The Hsia boys were taught the Chinese classics by private tutors at home, and later sent to a progressive high school in Changde. After high school, both went abroad to study law in Japan, which was considered the highest center of learning in Asia. They were among the first wave of students who went overseas to 'drink foreign ink.' When the Hsia brothers finished their studies and returned home, they were given heroes' welcome. The townspeople lined up in the street exploding firecrackers and playing gongs. It was the reception fit for an arriving mayor or high official. From then on, the Hsias were acknowledged as the First Family in town."

"I knew little about my father, except that he was the principle of the high school. His death came so suddenly and everyone was devastated. Still, no one wanted to talk about him. If he had not died so young, my life would not have been such a tragic mistake."

"As I reached old age, my past began to come back to me. Despite the painful memories, I felt a need to know something about my father, but there was no one to talk to, your Nai Nai and your mother had already passed away."

"Suddenly, my life was changed by a letter I received from my nephew in our old home town. He sent me the clipping of a newspaper article, written by a Communist historian, on the early development of Communism in the region. The article stated that during the Communist uprising in Hunan in 1927, the People's (Communist) Army executed the members of a local gang known as 'The Six Gentlemen' and my father was listed as one of them. This news really upset me because I knew it was not true. My father died in 1925, not 1927, and he was killed not by Communists but by a Nationalist warlord. I wrote a letter to the author telling him of his mistakes and demanded a public apology. The man wrote back and challenged me to prove that he was wrong. By tradition, to clear the family name and restore honor to one's ancestor is the noblest of personal achievements. That's why I decided to devote the rest of my life to finding the truth about my father."

By then, I was already seventy years old, but I was healthy in body and in spirit. I got on the train and went back to the hometown I had not seen since I was a teenager. Of course, the town had completely changed; I could not recognize the place. I visited relatives and the high school where my father worked, but no one remembered the events that had happened more than half a century ago. Besides, there was so much red tape that blocked the way. But I did not give up."

"I had a nephew named Chen who was a retired government official. He still had many connections in government and knew how to get around the red tape. Chen helped me locate several prominent Communists who had personally known my father. One was the son of the late Lin Baijue (also known as Lin Zuhan), who was a high ranking member of the Politburo and a close friend of my father. The elder Lin was one of the founders of the Communist party, a pre-eminent statesman and a Secretary of the Treasury. He had represented the Communist party in peace negotiations with the Nationalists (mediated by U.S. ambassador Patrick Hurley) at the end of the Second World War."

"I went to see Lin's son. He was very cordial because he remembered my father, and he was eager to help me in my search for the truth. Lin gave me two important documents that helped me to unearth my father's role in the revolution. One was Lin Baijue's diary written while he was a student in Japan, the other was a historical document on the Wuchang uprising of 1913, which launched the movement that eventually toppled the Qing government."

"With Lin Baijue's diary in hand, I went to the local newspaper agency and the police bureau and convinced them that I had an important mission. After much cajoling, I succeeded in recovering several original newspaper articles published in 1925 documenting my father's death. The story had appeared in local as well as major newspapers in Shanghai and Tianjin. I also found two very old people, a former teacher and a janitor who remembered my father. At my request, each of them wrote an article about my father's contributions to the town and the circumstances surrounding his death. I spent three years making long journeys to my hometown, riding on trains where there was standing room only, visiting with officials, relatives and people on the streets. I gradually came to understand something about my father's life, his dreams and the contributions he made to the community. I wrote an article based on the documents and oral histories I had collected and had it published in the same local newspaper that my father had founded more than half a century earlier."

Here is what my Aunt wrote:

> *My father, Hsia Guorui (his other name was Hsia xigui) was born in 1886 to a merchant family during the late Qing dynasty. After graduation from the Normal School in Changde, he and his older brother were sent to study law in Japan on government scholarships. The period 1905-1911 was, for my father, a time of intellectual and political awakening. He was awed by the scientific and technological*

progress in Japan and by the success of the political reforms there. He was convinced that China could do the same if we followed the path of the radical revolutionary movement headed by Dr. Sun Yat-sen.

In 1911, my father returned home to China and immediately threw himself into the underground revolutionary movement together with his good friends Lin Baijue and Jiang Yiwu. The three men were born in the same year, in the same town, and went to the same school. Jiang was the leader and organizer of the Wuchang uprising; my father was the editor of the organization's newspaper "People's Journal." Before they could launch their revolt, however, there was a leak; 600 revolutionaries were captured and executed. My father, Lin and Jiang were able to escape. The Wuchang uprising, although ill-fated, was the catalyst which ignited nationwide revolts by local armies and provincial assemblies, and eventually brought down the Qing dynasty.

After the establishment of a republican government, Sun Yat-sun relinquished the presidency to the powerful warlord general Yuan Shi Kai. Yuan believed that China needed an absolute central authority to unite the country, and he proceeded to restore the monarchy and to install himself as emperor. The act was met with public fury; the entire country rose up in protest. My father joined Jiang, Lin and other revolutionaries in organizing military attacks, called "the second revolution" against the dictator. Yuan ruthlessly suppressed the movement, and many of its leaders were assassinated. Jiang was arrested and executed, while Lin and my father escaped to Japan.

During my father's second visit to Japan, he concentrated on the study of education, while Lin studied economics. A brief account of their activities can be found in Lin's diary, which covered the period from Aug 1913 to September 1917. These two men were the closest of friends, they regularly had dinners at each other's homes, and they went on outings and visits together. The diary mentioned their attending meetings together, although the nature and place of the meetings were never disclosed.

In Lin's memoir, published later in his life, he attributed his ideological progression from patriotism to socialism to the influence from Li Dazhou whom he met in Japan. Li had earned the reputation as a progressive writer, and had given Lin a lot of literature on Marxist theory. At the time, Japan had just undergone its own political and literature reform, and socialism was in vogue. The Chinese students often attended meetings sponsored by the Japanese Socialist Party which was established in 1906. The earlier Chinese literature on anarchism and socialism were translated from Japanese to Chinese by these students.

The Chinese students in Japan had formed a closely-knit group and looked out for one another. Lin had mentioned in his memoir that Li Dazhou had once pawned his raincoat to help a friend pay his debt.

After my father, Lin Baijue and Li Dazhao had finished their studies and returned to China, their paths diverged. Lin Baijue plunged head-on into politics in the pursuit of his socialist ideals. In 1918, Li Dazhao was appointed head librarian at Peking University where he established the "Marxist Research Society." Together with Chen Duxiu, dean of Peking University, they attracted many progressive-minded young people, including Mao Zedong. In 1920, Li Dazhou and Chen Duxiu founded the Chinese Communist party in Shanghai and Lin Baijue became one of the earliest members. I have no information on whether my father had become a member as well. In 1927, the year when the Nationalists declared open war on Communists, Lin Baijue was sent to Moscow to study Marxism.

When my father returned to China in 1918, he found a nation divided by warlords. Dejected by the power

GRANDFATHER'S MICROSCOPE

struggles and political turmoil, my father devoted the remaining years of his life (1918-1925) to the education of the younger generation. He became head of the department of education, and principal of the high school (the place of highest learning in his hometown). He helped to establish a women's normal school, and became the founding editor of the local newspaper. In his spare time, he practiced law while his brother served as the judge in the local court.

It was later said that my father was always on the side of the poor, the illiterate and the underprivileged. During trials, he sat in his seat hunched over in deep concentration with his face buried in his hands. When he finally rose to address the court, his speech was so eloquent and powerful that he never lost a case. Although he came from a wealthy family, he despised the accumulation of wealth at the expense of poor people.

In the high school, my father introduced the students to the world outside China and instilled the students with his vision of a united, progressive and democratic China. He placed great emphasis on modern sciences and health education. Father taught the young men and women to be free thinkers, to better themselves through education, to be unselfish and to serve the people and the country. He encouraged his students to express their views, however bold.

He founded the first modern newspaper in town. In editorials, he emphasized his belief in freedom of speech and attacked the corrupt government officials and warlords who had divided the country. He rallied against the evil customs of the old society, condemned foot-binding and supported women's rights.

As student enrollment increased in the school, there was shortage of classrooms. My father sold land inherited from his father and used the money to build additional classrooms. The new buildings were fashioned in the

Japanese style, as they provided better light and ventilation than traditional Chinese architecture. But his love and admiration for Japan would soon turn into hatred following the May 4th incident of 1919, when students in Beijing gathered in Tiananmen Square to protest against Japan's aggression. (See addendum at end of chapter)

My father responded to the May 4th movement with fervor and devotion as he led the students in anti-Japan, and anti-warlord demonstrations. In just a few years, he had opened the eyes of the town's people, and he was called by his students "the revered teacher and leader of our generation."

In 1922, Sun Yat-sen reorganized the Nationalist Party (Guomindang) and allowed communists to become members. They were preparing to launch the "Northern Expedition" with the goal of reuniting the country. My father was an enthusiastic supporter and he rallied young men in his town including his own nephew and sent them to Guandong to join the Northern Expedition's Revolutionary Army.

In 1925, a certain division of Nationalist troops, headed by a warlord General Tung, came to Hunan on the pretense that they were on their way to join the Northern Expedition. Instead, the troops settled in our hometown, occupied the high school, fed on the drought-stricken people, robbed and raped. The General, with the consent of six powerful local gentry, nicknamed the "Six Gentlemen," demanded that the townspeople pay a large sum of tax money to support the army. My father rallied teachers, students and townspeople to protest to the local government and ask the army to leave. The protest and demonstrations went unheeded. My father then wrote a series of newspaper articles to denounce the warlord.

Friends warned him about the danger of offending a powerful, anti-leftist warlord. Some friends advised him to stay away for a while. But his answer was: "I have gone through revolutions and battles and seen blood shed and comrades die. What fear do I have for one man and one army? It would be shameful if I run away and surrender to evil. Who would speak for the people? How would our young people learn to respect law and justice? If I die, I will have set a good example and be worthy of the company of Jiang and other comrades who died for the revolution!"

On March 28, 1925, my father was arrested by soldiers and taken to the court presided over by the warlord General. The General told my father to apologize and to admit his crime. My father's reply was: "What is the crime of serving the people?" Tung then shouted: "Aren't you afraid to die?" My father replied: "I am willing to die for the people." Then my father launched into a speech condemning Tung for his crimes. Tung was so infuriated that he ordered my father to be immediately taken to the execution ground outside the South City Gate.

Upon hearing the news of my father's arrest, the students and teachers gathered at the school ground and held an emergency meeting. They marched en masse to the warlord's headquarters to demand my father's release, but it was too late. After the execution, people gathered in the streets and wept openly. The news of my father's death spread far and wide, and incited outrage amongst the national news media. During the following weeks, newspapers in Shanghai and Tianjin reported the event and protested the violation of human rights.

Here is how one newspaper article ended the story: "Hsia's oldest daughter, upon hearing of her father's death, returned home from Shanghai where she was attending college. Ignoring personal danger, the young woman stormed into the Mayor's office and handed him a hand-written letter of grievance. She demanded that the mayor punish the murderer. Collectively, the influential people in town made *an appeal to the provincial government and demanded justice. The public outcry and criticism from the press throughout the country eventually drove Tung's army out of town."*

At the time of my father's death, Mao Zedong was organizing workers, farmers and students in Changsha and was starting a revolution against landowners and foreigners. The spring of 1927 was the height of the Communists' power; Hunan was under siege. The Communists occupied my hometown and executed the "Six Gentlemen" and other property owners. Shortly afterwards, the local army, together with landowners, retaliated and killed thousands of leftist students and peasant leaders. Fifty years later, the party historian accurately recounted the event of the Communist uprising, but he had made the mistake of listing my father as one of the "Six Gentlemen."

I am writing this article to correct the mistake made by the historian and to present to the world the contributions and sacrifices my father made for his people and his country. I hope it will give a measure of comfort to my father's spirit in heaven.

First Aunt continued: "After my article was published in the newspaper, I went to the house of the official who had wrongly accused my father of being a tyrannical thug. I stood at the door and handed him my article. He had no choice but to make a public apology. Since then, my father's life story has been reprinted in several newspapers and magazines and even aired on local TV. We were not successful in getting his name on the list of "Martyrs of the Revolution" that were honored in Beijing this year (there were too many of them), but I am satisfied with what I have accomplished. Your grandfather is finally vindicated."

* * *

After hearing First Aunt's story, I was deeply moved. I genuinely admired her for her courage and determination in taking on such a formidable task in her old age. It's ironic that First Aunt, the lazy and unpromising child, the woman who had disgraced the family, had finally accomplished what the Chinese called *zeng qi;* she had honored and avenged her father. She had also set an example for the next generations to follow.

I could not help but feel that my grandfather's tragic death was avoidable. His surviving family members must have blamed him for his recklessness. But at the same time, I could truly relate to him and his stubborn, unyielding Hunan temperament.

Why had the poignant story of my grandfather's life remained hidden for so long? The answer lies in the dangerous political climate that has plagued China for much of the past century. At the time when my family lived under Nationalist rule and the Japanese occupation, no one dared to mention Grandfather's name because of his ties with the Communists. Even after the Communist liberation, the general atmosphere was so unpredictable that people avoided doing anything that would attract attention. In order to survive, you had to blend in with the crowd, to dress, talk, and behave the same as everyone else. During the Cultural Revolution, people who were outstanding or just different, were singled out for persecution. Even the old Communist Marshals, including my grandfather's good friend General He Long, who had fought and won the revolution, were persecuted as well. My aunt had to wait until the Cultural Revolution was over before she could embark on her quest for the truth.

In May 1995, on the seventieth anniversary of Grandfather's death, I went to my hometown, to symbolically sweep Grandfather's grave and to pay respect to his memory. The Director of Foreign Affairs at the Hunan Medical College, Dr. Yang, arranged a van, a driver, and asked several colleagues to accompany me on this trip. It was a leisurely two-day journey that took us along the banks of meandering rivers, and among endless green rice fields dotted by farmers and water buffalos, scenes that had not changed for centuries.

As our van entered Lixian, a quaint and prosperous little town, I was swept up by feelings of joy, sorrow, and nostalgia. This was the place where my ancestors had lived, worked, dreamed, suffered and died. I could still feel the ghosts of their hopes, aspirations, loves, hates, and sufferings lingering in the air.

I was met by the local party officials who took me to the First Municipal High School, now rated as the best school in the region. The classrooms were housed in tall new buildings; the library and the science laboratories were well equipped. The school principal and his staff were delighted to have the new information about my grandfather. They had no record on him beyond the fact that he had served as the school principal in 1925.

The officials took me to the execution ground at the South City Gate where my grandfather, and subsequently, many Communist members were killed. They had since built a Martyr's Memorial Park next to the execution site. I laid a wreath of flowers in front of the tall white monument, bowed three times and burned a bunch of incense, feeling all the while that Grandfather was standing twenty feet away, watching and smiling.

The year 1996 marked the ninetieth anniversary of the founding of the First Municipal High School. The school celebrated the occasion with a special memorial journal that contained old photographs and essays contributed by alumni. There was one photograph, taken in 1920, depicting a Japanese-styled building. Could this be the one built by my grandfather?

I wrote an article about my grandfather's life for the special occasion. I also contributed a sum of money to the school for the establishment of the "Outstanding Teachers' Award" in my grandfather's name.

Grandfather is no longer a "nameless martyr." His portrait is now hanging on the wall in the corridor of the administrative building, amongst the pictures of those who succeeded him.

Mei laying a wreath for Grandfather before the Martyr's memorial monument in her ancestral town of Lixian. 1997.

Addendum on May 4th movement: In 1914, Japan took advantage of the outbreak of the First World War and declared war on Germany. Japanese troops then seized Qingdao which was formerly leased to Germany. Next, Japan issued the infamous "Twenty-one Demands:" Japan wanted to takeover all the privileges previously extended to Germany in Shandong; to control the ports, railroad and mining rights in Manchuria, inner Mongolia, southeast coast and the Yantze Valley; China must appoint Japanese nationals to be consultants in all military, political, and financial arenas; the Chinese police department was to be run jointly with

Japanese; and half of the weapons used by Chinese military had had to be purchased from Japan. Furthermore, China was not allowed to lease or sell any sea ports or territories to other foreign countries. Even though the demand was clearly a prelude to annexation of China, it was accepted by the warlord premier Duan Qirue in exchange for personal favor.

When the First World War ended in 1918, the Chinese people were anticipating international justice and termination of colonial occupation. But they were shattered by news from the postwar peace negotiation at Versailles that Britain, France and Italy had signed a secret treaty to place in Japanese hands Germany's claim in Shandong in exchange for Japanese naval assistance against Germany during the war.

Chinese hostility to the news was extreme and culminated in a nationwide anti-Japanese movement, and boycott of Japanese goods. On May 4th 1919, thousands of students from fourteen colleges and universities led by students of Peking University, "Beida" in abbreviation, gathered at the Tiananmen Square, marched on the streets and clashed with the police. The May 4th incident had resulted in an unprecedented awakening of national consciousness and a fervent patriotic movement. Chinese students studying abroad, particularly in Japan, were greatly agitated by news from Beijing. They demonstrated in Tokyo and clashed with the police. More than half of the Chinese students left Japan en mass. At home, they became powerful spokesmen for the anti-Japanese movement.

The Chinese delegates at the Versailles were bombarded by telegrams of protests from Chinese at home and overseas. When the Chinese public learned that the government had secretly instructed the Paris delegates to sign the peace treaty, there were again massive violent demonstrations. Chinese students and demonstrators blockaded the headquarter of the delegation at a Paris hotel to prevent them from attending the signing ceremony. The May 4th movement ended victoriously with China refusing to sign the peace treaty.

Events following the Versailles treaty had revealed to the world Japan's ambition to dominant the Asian Pacific region. During the Washington Conference in 1922, the delegates took measures to limit the extensive Japanese naval build up and to protect U.S. interest in the Pacific. Japan agreed to relinquish the 21 demands of 1915, and to restore Qingdao to China as well as the railroad rights seized from Germany.

At the outset, the May 4th incident was simply a student demonstration against colonialism. After the May 4th incident, the emphasis shifted from external (anti-Japan) to internal domestic issues and the leadership shifted from Beida students to their teachers.

The Chancellor of Peking University, Tsai Yuanpei, had been regarded as the greatest liberal educator of his time. His emphasis was on the introduction of western culture and democracy, preservation of national quintessence and creation of a new civilization. He was able to recruit a new breed of scholar elites newly returned from studying abroad; prominent among them were Chen Duxiu, dean of school of letters and Li Dazhou, chief librarian, co-founders of the Chinese Communist Party; Hu Shi, professor of philosophy; Liang Qichow and Lu Xun, professors of literature. Although diverse in their philosophical and political believes, they had collectively led the new generations of Chinese youth to critically re-examine the traditional social and cultural issues such as family structures, customs, code of ethics, interpersonal relationship and the place of women. For thousands of years, the Chinese behavior had been dictated by rigid rules adopted mainly from Confucianism with modifications by the rulers to suit their own purposes. Now the new intellectuals were leading the way to powerful cultural and political reforms, one of which was the birth of Chinese Communism.

Chapter 17

YUAN, THE SPIRITUAL LINK

In the employee's dining hall at the Hunan Medical College, I was ushered into the VIP room. The college's top administrators had invited me to a banquet to express their appreciation for my contributions.

We started dinner with six kinds of cold appetizers, followed by three steaming soups and twelve hot entrees. There was a whole fish soup cooked in hot pepper and a rare purple spice; a soup of black-skinned chicken cooked in medicinal herbs; and a whole steamed winter melon, hollowed out and stuffed with spareribs, dried shrimp and mushrooms. They brought out a dish of eels sautéed with cucumbers, followed by frog legs cooked with hot pepper and bamboo shoots. Some of the dishes I had never seen before, but the taste was authentic Hunan cuisine. My favorite was a familiar dish of my childhood, Hunan December ham sautéed with garlic sprouts and hot peppers. To go with these scrumptious dishes, we drank "drunken devil's liquor," a famous local brew contained in an old-fashioned clay bottle. When the seal was broken, the room was instantly filled with a potent, pungent bouquet.

Everyone at the table was in a jovial, festive mood. All of the college administrators were locals, born and raised in Hunan, and graduates of the Hunan Medical College. They were chatting in a Hunan-accented Mandarin, the official language spoken by my parents. The tastes and sounds of Hunan brought back long forgotten memories, immense warmth and nostalgia.

Sitting to my left was the dean of basic sciences, a man by the name of Xie. He was a middle-aged, distinguished looking man with elegant manners. During the course of casual conversation, Dr. Xie told me that one of his relatives had lived in Taiwan for many years.

"What was he doing in Taiwan?" I asked, between morsels of food.

"He was the Mayor of Keelung."

At that point, I drew a sharp breath and dropped my chopsticks. On hearing the name "Xie" and "Mayor of Keelung," I felt as if I had been struck by lightening. Without thinking, I blurted out the question:

"Was he buried on top of the foothill overlooking the Keelung Harbor?"

"Why yes, did you know him?" He was as shocked as I was.

"Yes, I knew him because he had saved me forty years ago!"

Chinese people have a way of remembering favors (as well as grudges) and would find ways to repay them. Otherwise the debt would forever weigh on their conscience. Throughout my adult life, I had regarded Mr. Zhang and Mayor Xie as the benefactors to whom I owed everything. When I first arrived at Keelung, lost and penniless, the two men had given me food and shelter. At the time, I was only twenty years old and was not given to introspection. I took their kindness as the customary generosity and loyalty characteristic of our people. My father was never hesitant to help his friends who were in need. But I had been troubled all my life by the thought that these two men had gone out of their way for a total stranger like me. Even though I had never met the Mayor in person and he probably didn't even remember me afterwards, I felt deeply indebted to him all my life.

All I knew about Mr. Zhang, whom I called Uncle Zhang, was that he had been an old family friend, highly intelligent and cultivated. We never had what might be called an intimate conversation, and I knew nothing about his past. He was living alone in Taiwan, and if he had a family, he must have left them on the mainland like countless others had done. I knew even less about Mayor Xie. At the time, I was curious about these two men, but it would have been against my upbringing and my timid nature to ask questions. So I kept them to myself.

After I had gone to the U.S., I kept up a correspondence with Uncle Zhang. He left the Mayor's office after a few years, and took up a post teaching Chinese history at a university in Taichung. He died a few years later, in his mid-fifties, of lung cancer; he was a heavy smoker. In his last letter to me, Uncle Zhang said he had left some books for me as souvenirs. Somehow I had never received those books. Now I wonder what those books might have been, and I would pay anything to have them today.

Thirty years later, when I first returned from the U.S. to Taiwan, I had tried to find whatever trace was left of Mr. Zhang. I inquired about him in Taichung where he had taught, but no one knew of him. The Hunan people I met had never heard of him either. My only hope was to find him in our old hometown.

On my trip back, I received two historical documents. One was a directory listing all the names of the teachers and students of the high school, from its first year. The other book, entitled "The Martyrs of Lixian," was given to me by the local government officials. I poured over these two books, line by line, in hopes of finding some clues about the mysteries that had plagued me all my life.

In the high school directory, my grandfather's name appeared among the list of principals. I found my father's name in the class of 1915. There were a number of students with the last name of Zhang, but no one had the same given name, Xiaoliu. According to the custom of the time, adult men were allowed to have two names, one given by his parents and one he chose for himself. It is entirely possible that Xiaoliu, meaning dawn willow, was not his original name. The only guess I could make was that Zhang Xiaoliu may have been a star student and devoted follower of my grandfather. He became a Nationalist while many of his classmates who had sworn loyalty to Communism had died as martyrs.

I learned from Dean Xie that his great-granduncle, the Mayor of Keelung, was from Changde, the city where my grandfather had gone to school and where he had had many friends. I still don't know whether Mayor Xie personally knew my grandfather.

Later, Dean Xie showed me a biography on the Mayor's life, compiled by family members and friends. It detailed his admirable characters and high moral standards, his illustrious career with the Nationalist government, and the contributions he made to the progress of Taiwan. Whatever their faults, his generation of Nationalist officials laid the foundation for today's Taiwan. I often wonder what it would have been like had these men remained in control of mainland China.

The book of the martyrs was a collection of poignant stories of the heroism of several hundred young men from our hometown who had joined the Communist party during its bloody early history. I was struck by the story of one man, named Luo Ting. In 1919, Luo went to study in France, where he joined the Communist Party. He returned home in 1925 and succeeded my grandfather as principal of the high school.

Luo established a branch of the Communist party in the school, and recruited many leftists. A year into his extraordinary career, fate intervened. He died in a boating accident at the age of 27. The year after his death, the Nationalists turned against the Communists. Many of Luo's followers were arrested and executed.

As far as I could determine, Luo Ting was the only person from our hometown who had gone to France during that period of time. In all probability, he was the person who had wanted my father to go to France with him, and who later lent him money to go to college. I doubted if my father ever had the chance to pay back this debt.

What an extraordinary coincidence that decades after these events, I would be drawn to my birthplace across thousands of miles and sit at a banquet table next to the Mayor's great-grandnephew! After I told the Dean about what happened in Keelung forty years ago, he was spellbound. Finally, we both agreed that we had *yuan* among us. The character of *yuan* is made up of "weave" on the left and "roots or origin" on the right. *Yuan* is a kind of predestined link, a mediator of meaningful relationships between two persons, or between a person and a place or an animal. *Yuan* is what draws people together; they drift apart when *yuan* runs out. When people say that their *yuan* with the dusty world has ended, it means that they are ready to accept death. We have a common saying:

> "*Yuan* brings strangers together across thousands of miles, without y*uan*, we face each other but remain strangers."

I saw in Professor Xie a kindred soul, a kind and intelligent man who loves Western classical music. When I left Hunan, I gave him my collection of music tapes and CDs, and then sent him a large package of classical music from the US. It was a small gesture that made me feel I was repaying my debt to his great-granduncle.

Considering the scope of the universe, it may be too egotistical to think that individual lives are so important as to call for divine intervention. I cannot imagine a god who pushes people around like puppets on a string. Still, there seem to be greater forces in the world that are beyond human understanding and control. In order to achieve our goals, talent and personal striving are not enough. We need the cooperation of that supernatural force, whether it is fate or chance or luck. In life I try my best, but leave the rest to fate.

"He who does not know fate cannot be a superior man."(Confucius)

Staff and graduate students of the Anatomy Department, Hunan Medical College. To Mei's right is Prof Xie Changsong (dean of basic sciences), further right is Prof. Wang Yanzhi who wrote the calligraphy and poems on this page and on the book cover.1996.

Chapter 18

THE SOUL BRIDGE

In old China, the New Year officially began on December 17th of the lunar calendar, when people would bribe the kitchen god and then send him off to heaven to give a good report on the status of the household. But the preparation for the New Year began long before the actual festive day. As the Chinese saying goes: "Food is heaven on earth," the national obsession with food reaches its peak during the New Year holiday. People would save money all year long to buy the special holiday foods, which were prepared according to family tradition. For example, my family made smoked meats in the Hunan fashion during the month of December, hence the name "December meats." Slabs of pork, chicken, duck and fish were marinated in salt and spices, then hung on a rod in the rickshaw shed and smoked over smoldering wood dust until they were blackened and stiff as boards. After cooking, the meats turned a deep, translucent pink with an incredibly pungent smoky taste.

Around the New Year, we could also expect an entirely

new suit of clothes. My mother would buy bolts of fabrics from the silk shop and summon a tailor to the house. The tailor, a short man who walked with a limp, would set up shop on a makeshift sewing table in a corner of the living room. With nimble hands, he cut the fabrics according to our measurements and sewed them on his hand-cranked sewing machine. A yellowing photograph taken by my father on New Year's Day of 1935 shows a line of Liu children, arranged in descending size, wearing identical new blue satin padded gowns.

New Years Day photo taken by Father.
From right to left: Lan, Mei, Na, and Yisheng.
Circa 1934.

For good luck, every family had to hang spring scrolls on either side of the front door. On long pieces of red paper, my father would write any number of good luck phrases, such as "peace and joy in the four seas," "long life and prosperity," and other personal messages and poems. Because my father was well known for his fine calligraphy, he had taken on the task of writing the spring scrolls for relatives and neighbors when he was a young man.

As the festival approached, people made special efforts to keep the general atmosphere of the household as pleasant as possible. They believed that a happy household would be pleasing to the gods and would bring good luck for the coming year. People refrained from fighting and arguing and words such as "death" and "doom" were forbidden. My sister Na who was accident-prone was not allowed to set the table. To break a rice bowl could bring about a gloomy outlook for the rest of the year.

On New Year's Eve, candles were lit and the large round dinner table was laid with ivory chopsticks, silver spoons and liquor glasses. One by one, courses of food were brought up from the kitchen. These savory dishes were what we called "mountain treasures and sea delicacies." The mountain dishes consisted of meat, poultry and other products such as bird's nest; the sea delicacies included the shark fin. Fish was considered twice lucky, because the word for "fish" has the same pronunciation *yu*, as the word for "plenty" although the characters are different. The fish was sometimes posed with its tail in its mouth, symbolizing the unbroken circle of luck for the coming year. It's the only dish that was not to be touched on New Year's Eve, so that the "plenty" could flow into the New Year.

We stood around the table as Father performed the annual ritual of ancestor worship. My father would gingerly pour liquor into the little glasses as he murmured the names of our departed ancestors. He was inviting them to come to the annual feast and to bestow blessings on the children. All of us stepped back with heads bowed waiting for the spirits to take the meal. After a few minutes of silence, Father stepped forward, took the glasses and poured drops of the liquor on the floor. This was a signal that the ghosts of the ancestors were departing and that we could take our seats and savor the heartiest meal of the year.

During dinner, Father would give his usual lecture, which he always began with a deep sigh. "Children! Think of the tumultuous time we are living in—wars, famine, and unrest. Millions of people have died, or are starving and homeless. We are so lucky to be together, alive and safe, with a roof over our heads and food on the table. This is blessing from heaven and good karma from our ancestors. So you must be thankful, be good, and study hard to deserve all the blessings given to us."

The next big item on the New Year's Eve agenda was the handing out of *hong bao*, or "red packets," which were basically our year-end bonus (usually coins or paper money wrapped in red paper). By custom, children had to kneel and kow-tow to the elders in order to receive their cash. Luckily, my parents considered kow-towing to be old fashioned and unsightly, so we only had to bow.

The New Year's festival was not complete without *renao* (heat and noise) or signs of prosperity generated by fireworks, dragon dance, carnivals, laughing and gambling. In our household, this was the only time of the year when children were allowed to gamble. We usually stayed up late playing dominos to our hearts' content. Father was the dealer, and we started out thinking that we could easily win the pile of money in front of him. But we soon found out that he was a crafty player, and we were no match for him. In a short time, our red packet money, which we had waited for all year long, were gone. Then we would sit back, look at one another and simultaneously burst out in tears. Father had no choice but to return our money because crying on New Year's Eve would bring bad luck. Maybe that's why to this day, there are no gamblers in our family.

On New Year's Day, with money in our pockets, Lan and I would go out and buy toys, wooden swords and firecrackers from the street vendors. Lan had learned how to play with fireworks from the boys on the street. She would light a firecracker in one hand and toss it like a hand grenade. For the large fireworks, she would set them on the ground, light them and run away before they exploded into the air, with the sparks falling like stardust. I was happy just to watch in awe. In China, people believed that fireworks had a magic ability to dispel ghosts and evil spirits. They were used to bring luck to the New Year, weddings, the opening of a new business or the completion of a new house. They were also used to mourn death, and to prevent sickness, drought and flood.

On the first day of the year, people would put on their best clothes and perform the ritual of *bynian*, bowing to their elders, friends and business partners. My father had a special outfit which he wore only on New Year's Day. It was a long Mandarin robe of brilliant blue satin, lined with red fox fur. When he wore it, he looked elegant and authoritative, like a high court official. Throughout the morning, my father's colleagues and friends would come filing through the gate. It was a wonderful sight to see these handsome young men clothed in padded silk gowns bowing to my father with both hands clasped in front of them, saying *gongxi, gongxi*, congratulations (for your impending good fortune).

The second day of the New Year was the traditional day for women to visit their own parents. But that custom had never applied to my mother, since her father was long dead and her mother had been living with us all those years. For my father, it was a day to remember the poor. He would ride in a rickshaw with a bag of coins on his lap and distribute the money to the beggars in the streets. To everyone, rich or poor, the New Year's holiday was a joyous occasion, one that had to be celebrated with passion. To work during the New Year would offend the gods and ancestors and bring bad luck. Shops were closed, some the entire month. People stayed home, eating, drinking, gambling or just relaxing with family and friends. For the farmers, this would be the only holiday they have for the entire year.

* * *

My last New Year's celebration on Chinese soil came about in 1997, at the conclusion of my teaching assignment in China and on my way to a quiet retirement in the United States. The final stop on my journey was my sister Lan's house in Hangzhou.

As my parents' caretaker, Lan was the custodian of much of my family's history, and I found her a precious source of information. My own memory of the family's past was like a broken movie. The first part, made up of images of when my parents were young, was clear, sharp, and for the most part full of warmth and happiness. After I left China, the story became sketchy, the scenes were incomplete and based on what was said and unsaid in letters from across the ocean. Since I returned to China, I had purposefully sought out friends and relatives to try to fill in the gaps.

When we sat down in Lan's tiny kitchen to begin preparing the New Year's feast, she began recounting our family's stories.

It wasn't long after my departure in 1949 that my family broke apart. After the Communists came to power, my father, then fifty years old, lost his lifelong job with the Custom's House, and could not feed his family. Four teenage siblings, two girls and two boys, joined the army. Only the youngest sister and a younger brother who was ill with tuberculosis stayed home. Nai Nai and Lin Ma returned to the family's home town and First Aunt went to work in Shanghai.

That year, Lan graduated from college and married an engineer with the approval of my parents. The two of them had much in common: both were talented in sciences as well as in art and music. Both landed in teaching jobs at Zhejiang University. My parents and the two youngest siblings moved in with Lan and her husband in a small apartment in Hangzhou. With the arrival of Lan's two daughters, the apartment was crammed.

Hangzhou, known as the "Venice of the East," was the kind of place my father had always dreamed about for his retirement. The first house they lived in was on the bank of the famous West Lake, where they could take walks and enjoy the scenery. My father learned to do household chores and helped take care of his granddaughters. Their lives were in good order until the country was devastated by a succession of man-made disasters: the great famine and the Cultural Revolution.

My family members managed to escape bodily harm during the Cultural Revolution. They were smart enough to lay low and not to attract attention. But my father had to sweep the streets, and Lan's two college-aged daughters were forced out of school and sent to work in the countryside. For the New Year, now called the Spring Festival, the siblings still managed to gather at Lan's house. They would travel many weary hours by train, each bringing a small parcel of some precious delicacy that they had managed to assemble through ingenuity and resourcefulness: perhaps a pound of ham, or a bag of peanuts. The money and food packages I sent home helped to make Spring Festival more joyous. No matter what terrible times they were living in, they still managed to keep our family tradition by gathering together for a *tan yuan fan* (union meal), making "heat and noise," being cheerful and saying *gongxi* in anticipation of better times ahead. These festivals were what tied the family together. In times of anxiety, depression, and even hopelessness, they always had one another and our family traditions.

During the Cultural Revolution, my mother started slipping away. Diabetes and glaucoma took away her sight. My normally reticent mother became excitable, talkative, and paranoid. Then she grew weak and lost the use of her limbs. Finally she became bed-ridden, incontinent and her mind slipped into a dark, incomprehensible world. She died after six long years of lingering illness. After her death, my father grew increasingly lonely and his health began to fail as well. He lost his appetite and the ability to walk up the stairway. During this time, there was a dramatic change in the political climate in China: Chairman Mao died, and the Gang of Four, who were blamed for much of the excesses of the Cultural Revolution, were imprisoned. Hope for a better life was in the air, but it all came too late for my parents.

According to tradition, the responsibility of caring for elderly parents and younger siblings normally fell to the eldest son. Because we were a gender-equal family, Lan and I always knew that one day we would be given these responsibilities. Since I was no longer there, the burden fell on Lan and her husband. My brother-in-law, Wang Ruze, was more attentive and devoted to my parents than my own three brothers. Lan and her husband never complained openly, but everyone knew that taking care of invalid parents was a terrible burden.

After I fled China, I was not able to go home and visit my parents until almost 30 years later. In 1978, not long after President Nixon's visit to China, a medical group had managed to get permission to visit hospitals in several large cities, including Hangzhou. Members of this group were Chinese

American doctors, many were my schoolmates in Taiwan, all had roots in China. I jumped on the chance to join the group, since at that time individuals were still not allowed to visit China. I left China when I was twenty years old; and now I was forty-nine, and my father eighty-three.

Seeing him was like a dream! As I ascended the dark stairway of Lan's apartment, I saw an elderly, white-haired man standing by the door. I did not recognize him. Who was this thin and frail old man? Surely not my father! Not the robust, middle-aged patriarch that I remembered, larger than life and seemingly invincible. After a few minutes looking at me, he asked in a quivering whisper:

"Is that you Mei-er (Mei-child, my nickname)?" I nodded, tears streaming down my face. I was speechless. It was not our custom to embrace.

Several hours later, Father said to me:

"Now I recognize you! You are the same as I remember you! Only your eye-glasses fooled me!" (I had a pair of large blue-tinted glasses). Later in the evening, I overheard him muttering to himself, citing a favorite poem: "One moment in this spring night is worth a thousand pieces of gold."

Lan told me that two weeks before my arrival, our father became seriously ill with what started out as a cold and turned into something like pneumonia. They feared that he would not live to see me. Everyone was so relieved that he got over his illness.

During my visit, Lan's house was filled to overflowing with our siblings. They had all made long journeys by train and slept on the floor in Lan's apartment. Not being used to camping out, I stayed in a downtown hotel. There was my first younger brother Yisheng, a math teacher in high school, and my youngest sister Yuan, a biology teacher. Each had brought along a child whom I had never seen. This was also the first time I met Lan's husband and her two daughters, Xiaolan and Tong.

Family outing on West Lake, Hangzhou, after three decades of separation. From left to right: Yuan (youngest sister), Fong (half sister), Lan, Mei, Lien (half sister) and Yisheng. 1978.

First family reunion dinner in 30 years, in Lan's house in Hangzhou. Front, from right to left: Tong, Lan, Father, and Mei. Back: Xiaolan. 1978.

I remember sitting opposite my father as he lay on his rattan recliner. I felt inconsolably sad and bereaved. My heart was bursting with intense feelings of love, loss and regret. I had accumulated oceans of words, but none would come out. I had to suppress my emotions, fearing that my grief would make him sad and damage his health. The only thing that I could clearly get across to him was that I was really happy to see him, and at the same time very sad that Mother was not there anymore. I talked briefly about my children, but said nothing about my divorce

For a few days, my father, who had been fragile and suffering from loss of appetite, became invigorated. He supervised the preparation of meals and watched with delight as we enjoyed the hearty food. At one point, we had to restrain him from having his second *jiaozi*(pork dumplings) for fear that his digestive system would not be able to handle it. We wanted him to live a long life and to enjoy the good times ahead. On the day I left, Father took out a stethoscope and asked me to give him a physical examination. "Can I live to be ninety?" he asked me. I found his heart beat fast and weak, his lungs clear, and his legs mottled and cold. I said, "sure, no problem."

Six months after I returned to the U.S., I got a letter from Lan telling me that Father had passed away suddenly. It was an apparent heart attack, quick and clean, no one had suspected that he had any heart trouble. They held a memorial service, and all the children and some grandchildren attended. After the service, the family divided up his meager possession and everyone got to keep a small souvenir. My brothers inherited Father's clothes, his blue satin fur-lined Mandarin robe went to Lan's husband. Na got his leather trunk. I got a bunch of precious old photographs and a paper weight made of jade.

Just as it was impossible for me to imagine the anguish and suffering endured by my relatives in China, it was equally difficult for them to imagine my sense of loss, loneliness and guilt. I wished I had been in the company of my parents for all those years, to talk to them as an adult, to ask them questions which I wouldn't dream of asking as a child, and to personally care for them in their old age. I wished my children could have known their grandparents and had the kind of loving relationship I now have with my own grandchildren. I wished that my parents had the chance to visit me in my new world and be awed by the wonders of America.

"How could our fates be so different?" was a question my siblings asked me.

As a scientist, I reject the idea of fate; it is a superstition, pure and simple. But I couldn't help wondering whether our lives are already determined, in some major way, at the time of birth.

For some mysterious reason, the fortuneteller's prediction that my life would be underscored by stormy events, every twenty years a cycle, had come true. When I was twenty years old, I was forced to abandon my family in a flight from Communism; at the age of forty, I lived through a devastating divorce; and at the age of sixty, another upheaval, another flight would take me half-way around the world, but this time in search of myself.

As I reflected on my fate, I saw the choices I had made that had put me on a different path from the rest. The critical point was when I had decided to leave my family and everything that was familiar and go to Taiwan. I took a leap in the dark and didn't know where I was landing. Going to American was something I had never dreamed of.

Of all the family, I was given a choice. In choosing, I would lose a large part of myself, but in return would be granted an opportunity no one dared to dream of in China. Not only would I escape disaster, but I would be given the freedom to choose whatever I wanted to do and wherever I wanted to live. A new world opened to me and my children. I used to ask my children if they would have liked to be born in China. They would always make a disgusting face and say, "yechhh!" They were not Chinese, they said, but Americans. It came as no surprise that all three married Caucasians.

When I was forty years old, I made my second critical choice, to take my life into my own hands. History had repeated itself, and I had experienced the same marital problems as my mother before me. But, thanks to her warnings, I was prepared, I had a profession. After overcoming a devastating divorce, I became a completely different person: independent and adventurous. I chose to do research in one of the most difficult areas in medicine, and dared to challenge the established dogma. I thrived on exploration and adventure. I wandered across the globe as my fancy took me. My home was wherever I happened to be at the moment.

In every city I lived and worked, I talked myself into believing that I would stay. I would buy and re-model a house and furnish it with good furniture. But in a few years' time, something would happen and I would have to move on. No matter how hard I tried, it seemed that I could never fit in anyplace. I was forever trying to call a place "home" while wondering where my "real home" was.

If my place was not in America, perhaps it was in China, I thought. But when I finally went back to live in China, I got a culture shock. I realized that I was more American in my thinking and behavior than I had realized. Also, China was no longer the place I remembered. The city where I grew up was totally rebuilt and unrecognizable. Great changes had taken place socially and culturally, and the way people behaved and lived their lives was totally alien to me. I found that I could not fit into China anymore.

In America, even though I think and act like an American, I am considered a foreigner, because I look and speak differently. Half-way around the world where I look and speak the same as everyone else, they still consider me a foreigner.

In Taiwan, they called me a "Mainlander." On the Mainland, they classify me as "Overseas Kindred," a guest.

But the most distressing feeling I had while living in China was a new kind of homesickness I hadn't experienced before. This time, I missed my children and I missed everything about America.

How differently things have turned out for my sisters! They have been living in the same neighborhoods and holding the same jobs all their lives. They have roots and life-long friendships. Whenever they step outside of their front doors, they are greeted by old colleagues and former students. Now that they are retired, they are living comfortably on government pensions. They engage in group activities with their old friends: practicing *tai chi* in the morning and rehearsing for singing performances in the afternoons. With the rapid improvement of economic and social conditions in China, they now have everything they wanted. They have finally come to realize that not everyone who went abroad got what they wanted. I hope this is some consolation for the difficult lives they have had and I hope they no longer feel regret for not having had the same opportunities as I.

Despite all odds, my sisters have managed to accomplish much in their lives. Even though we were very different as children (Lan was gifted in arts and literature, Na and I were good students of science, while our youngest sister Yuan was a talented dancer), in the end, we all became teachers in scientific fields: medicine, biology, physics, chemistry, mathematics and engineering. We achieved what our patriotic father and grandfather had hoped for us: to master subjects necessary in the building of a new and strong China. We also took our mother's advice to heart, to "eat whatever you like."

I think the reason that we all did similar things in our lives is that we all carry, not only the same genes, but the same hopes and dreams of the people who lived before us. They passed on to us their gifts, their faults, their dreams and values. From our mother's side, we inherited a quick mind and an unyielding spirit. Our father gave us his artistic, temperamental, and romantic inclinations. And from Lin Ma, although she was not related to us by blood, we learned about loyalty, devotion and stoicism. Despite the vast difference in our fates and circumstances, and decades of separation, we all arrived at the same end. We were united by a soul bridge that stretched in time through the centuries and across the mountains and oceans that separated us.

What had helped to unite us were those family rituals and meals shared together during good and bad times. I would always remember our father at the dinner table, a glass of wine in hand, telling stories, sharing his optimistic views or reminding us of our blessings and our responsibilities.

During the years of my exile, I had been carrying on a continuous dialogue with the spirits of my ancestors. Whenever I sat down to a good meal, I would make a toast to them. Whenever I was confronted with a moral or intellectual dilemma, I would seek their advice and they always gave me the right answer. I came to respect that vast, mysterious reservoir of knowledge and modes of communication that lay beneath our consciousness.

I have come to realize that every major step I took in life was to fulfill my ancestors' collective dreams: my father's Yale dream, my mother's feminist dream and my grandfather's dream of a better world. I believe it was my subconscious fascination with my grandfather's microscope that made me choose pathology, a profession that uses the microscope as its primary tool. It was the spirit embodied in my grandfather's microscope that had guided me throughout my life.

Edwards Brothers Malloy
Thorofare, NJ USA
July 19, 2012